Great Canadian Political Cartoons

1915 to 1945

CHARLES

AND

CYNTHIA HOU

MOODY'S LOOKOUT PRESS
VANCOUVER, BRITISH COLUMBIA

Moody's Lookout Press
Vancouver, British Columbia

Canadian Cataloguing in Publication Data

Hou, Charles, 1940-
  Great Canadian political cartoons, 1915 to 1945

Includes bibliographical references and index.
ISBN 0-9680016-4-5

  1. Canada--Politics and government--20th century--
Caricatures and cartoons. 2. Editorial cartoons--Canada--
History--20th century. I. Hou, Cynthia, 1941- II. Title.
FC173.H692 2002   320.971'02'07   C2002-910707-5
F1026.4.H682 2002

Reprinted   2010

Cover by Echelon Design, based on a cartoon by Les Callan
Printed and bound in Canada by Hignell Book Printing

CONTENTS

Preface

"History is that which says, not what could have been or should have been, but what has been, no more, no less. It must call the good, good, and the bad, bad. It takes into account, of course, the ideas, the atmosphere, and the customs of each age. But it has not the right to alter the truth in any way, and even less to pardon everything."   Canon Lionel Groulx[1]

The country we know as Canada underwent great change in the three centuries that preceded the First World War. The "few acres of snow" colonized by France in the early 1600s became in turn a colony of Britain and a semi-independent Dominion within the British Empire. In the three decades that followed, Britain's power and influence in Canada would decline and Canada's independence and ties to the United States would increase. This transition, and the events of the war–interwar–war period, would be captured in a unique and often provocative way by the political cartoonists of the day, who did not hesitate to call the good, good, and the bad, bad.

The most fundamental change to take place during this thirty-year period was the growth of a distinct Canadian identity. The outbreak of the First World War in August of 1914 was the catalyst that spurred this growth. As a member of the British Empire Canada entered the war by default when Britain declared war on Germany. Many of its citizens eagerly volunteered to serve, and others were recruited under protest when conscription was eventually introduced.

The battles of Ypres, the Somme and Vimy, among others, brought Canadians together in a common cause. Some worked to support the war effort at home; others, from all parts of the country, fought side by side in Europe. The defeats and victories of the Canadians overseas were mourned and celebrated by those at home. The battle of Vimy Ridge in northern France held particular significance, and the Canadian victory there has been referred to as a national coming of age. After the war Canada's contribution to the war was recognized with a separate seat at the Peace Conference at Versailles and a separate seat in the newly formed League of Nations.

While many Canadians sacrificed their lives during the war, others made large profits supplying munitions and other goods to the armed forces. A tax on income was introduced to raise money for the war effort. Some of those who had profited from the war purchased knighthoods with their new fortunes, to the outrage of many.

In the years that followed the war labour unions fought to increase workers' share of the nation's wealth. Issues such as child labour, sweatshops, unemployment insurance and workmen's compensation also came to the fore. Women had played a significant role in the work force during the First

---

[1] Lionel Groulx, "Why we are Divided," an address delivered in Montreal on November 20, 1943, and published in translation by *L'Action Nationale*.

World War, and while the postwar years saw their influence in the workforce decline, their influence in public life increased.

The war was followed by a period of depression in the early 1920s and a period of prosperity in the mid to late 1920s. This period of prosperity was followed in turn by a prolonged worldwide depression in the 1930s. Many of those who had money lost it when the stock market fell on Black Tuesday, October 29, 1929. Unemployment was high and many men laboured for next to nothing in work camps or "rode the rods" from place to place in search of better prospects. Women were even less likely to find gainful employment.

Before the First World War there had been two major political parties in Canada, the Liberals and the Conservatives. After the war others came on the scene. Canada itself had changed. Industries had developed, population had shifted from rural areas to the cities, and further immigration had increased the diversity of groups within the country. The traditional parties no longer met all needs. The United Farmers and the Progressives became a major force in parts of the country. The Depression stimulated not only fringe parties with communist and fascist leanings, but parties with large followings such as the Cooperative Commonwealth Federation (CCF), the Union Nationale and the Social Credit Party. Some of these parties had a sizable impact on the mainstream Liberal and Conservative parties, which adopted some of their more popular and less radical ideas.

The foundations for a system of health care and social programs were laid in the war–interwar–war period. Doctors had traditionally treated most people at home. Poor people sought medical care as a last resort, and disease and mortality rates were high. The few hospitals that existed were run by charities. People began to press for more adequate health care for all. Other social concerns involved the problems of alcohol and drug addiction and support for the young, the elderly, the poor and the unemployed.

As a nation with an aboriginal population and two immigrant founding cultures, Canada had always faced problems of race and language. The language rights of French Canadians living outside Quebec had been reduced prior to the First World War and continued to be a point of contention between English and French Canadians. The latter saw little reason to fight for freedom in Europe when they were denied certain freedoms at home. The Conscription Crisis of the First World War fed bitter racial tensions and an antiwar sentiment in Quebec which would last through the Second World War. There were other problems as well. The educational system in Quebec had not kept pace with the demands of the twentieth century, and high school graduates who lacked fluency in English were often out of luck. French Canadians were under-represented in the economic sphere and in the civil service. Quebeckers resented not being able to conduct business in their own language, in their own province. The federal government took small steps toward bilingualism in the interwar period when postage stamps and currency appeared bearing both official languages.

Canada was not a nation of native people, English and French alone. Immigrants from many countries had come to Canada in the decades prior to the First World War. Immigration increased after the First World War then ground almost to a halt during the Depression. During both the First and the Second World Wars many immigrants from the countries with which Canada was at war were imprisoned, sent to detention camps, or otherwise had their rights restricted. Government policies dealt strictly with members of visible minorities and potential refugees seeking asylum in Canada. The atrocities of the Second World War would force Canadians to find better ways of dealing with such issues.

The First World War had greatly reduced Britain's political and economic power. After the war Britain was unable to invest as much time and money in the Dominions as it had before and was willing to give them greater independence. Canada's growing control over its own foreign policy was apparent during the Chanak crisis in Turkey in 1922, when Canada told Britain not to count on Canada's support if war were to break out in the region. In 1922 Canada also signed the Halibut Treaty with the United States without Britain's intervention. The 1926 Balfour Report gave the Dominions equal status with Britain and the right to establish foreign embassies. Canada's independence was officially recognized under the Statute of Westminster in 1931.

The void left by Britain was soon filled by the United States. Americans eagerly invested in Canada. They continued to see Canada as a source of raw materials for processing in their own country, and starting in 1935 sought increased free trade. The Americans also flooded Canada with their magazines, films and radio broadcasts. Concern over Americanization and immorality in the media led to censorship and restrictions, and to the formation of the Canadian Broadcasting Corporation. In 1940 Canada accepted the promise of American military protection offered by the Ogdensburg agreement, and in 1941 tied itself to the American economy through the Hyde Park agreement.

Following the First World War Canada had reduced its armed forces to an insignificant level and tried to keep out of international entanglements. In September of 1939 the Second World War broke out and the country could no longer isolate itself from the rest of the world. An unprecedented royal visit by King George VI and Queen Elizabeth in May and June of

1939 had strengthened Canada's loyalty to Britain, and Canadians once more found themselves fighting on foreign soil. Again there were crushing defeats and costly victories. Canadians fought, and were defeated, in the Battle of Hong Kong in December 1941. On the European front there was a disastrous attack on Dieppe, a successful campaign in Italy and France, and a grim advance through the Netherlands. At the end of the First World War Canada had seized the privileges of nationhood without assuming its responsibilities; as the Second World War came to an end its citizens had a better sense of what it meant to be Canadian and felt confident enough to play a role in international affairs. Canada, once a colony, had become a nation.

Many of the events and issues of the war–interwar–war period were chronicled in the form of political cartoons in hundreds of newspapers and magazines across the country. Major newspapers, which employed most of the cartoonists, tended to support the mainstream parties and a narrow range of social issues. Self censorship and official censorship sometimes limited political comment. Other publications promoted much less orthodox and sometimes radical views. The cartoons presented here are drawn from a wide variety of sources; a number, regardless of their source, do not meet today's standards of political correctness but are included for their historical value.

While the collection as a whole cannot provide a complete and unbiased history of Canada from 1915 to 1945, it does provide some intriguing insights into Canadian history and a graphic view of many of the concerns and attitudes people had at the time.

This book is dedicated to the many fine cartoonists
whose work appears in these pages.

ALL FOR THE EMPIRE'S DEFENCE
The Lion's cub bares his teeth.

When Britain declared war on Germany in August of 1914 her colonies were automatically at war. At the beginning of the war Canada's main contribution to the war effort was soldiers, but as the war progressed Canada's wealth, natural resources and manufactured goods were needed. The British Columbian, *New Westminster, 30 Aug 1915*

TWO CONCEPTIONS OF EMPIRE

POOR ONTARIO

Left. *As a colony of Britain Canada had little control over her foreign affairs. Opposition leader Wilfrid Laurier wanted Canada to attain independence and to shape her own foreign policy, while Prime Minister Borden wanted Canada to attain equal status within the British Empire. The Halifax Herald, 30 Jan 1915*
Right. *Prohibition became increasingly popular during the First World War. Aside from the old arguments against alcohol shown in this cartoon, scarce resources and a great deal of manpower were being wasted in the unnecessary production of liquor. The Pioneer, Toronto, 20 Aug 1915*

MAN — AND SUPERMAN

The German philosopher Nietzsche claimed that the evolutionary process produced an ideal race having superior physical and intellectual powers. In April of 1915 Canadian troops fought their first major battle of the war at Ypres in Belgium. The Germans launched the first poison gas attack in history against the Canadians and some French and Algerian troops. The Canadians suffered heavy losses but held their ground against the "superman." John Bull, *reprinted in* The Toronto Star Weekly, *16 Oct 1915*

THE KING OF CANADA

During the war some businessmen made large profits supplying materials for the war effort, while the farmers and labourers who produced the goods received little for their efforts. The Grain Growers' Guide, *Winnipeg, 3 Feb 1915*

CLEANING UP THE "DIRTY MESS"

In 1915 the Manitoba government was in need of a cleanup. Women such as Winnipeg's Nellie McClung believed that women voters would help rid politics of corruption and graft. Manitoba Free Press, Winnipeg, 9 Jul 1915

THE MILCH COW

This cartoon illustrates the Western Canadian belief that Eastern bankers, railway corporations and manufacturers profited by denying Western farmers lower interest rates, lower freight rates and free trade. **The** Grain Growers' Guide, *Winnipeg, 15 Dec 1915*

TABLES DE MULTIPLICATION

La méthode canadienne-française... et l'autre. (M. Arthur Hawkes, journaliste anglais, dit que les Canadiens-français ont adopté, dans leur lutte pour l'existence, ce qu'il appelle "la méthode du berceau.")

MULTIPLICATION TABLES. The French Canadian way... and the other way. (Mr. Arthur Hawkes, an English journalist, says that French Canadians have adopted, in their struggle for survival, "the method of the cradle.") [tr.] In 1911 the English had 112 births per 1000, while the French had 161. A significantly higher birthrate in French Canada helped counteract the growth of English Canada due to immigration. Le Nationaliste, *Montreal, 9 Jul 1916*

ALBERTA

THE SPIRIT OF THEIR FOREFATHERS

Vivent les Canadiens-Français.

Left. Women got the right to vote in Manitoba, Saskatchewan and Alberta in 1916, thanks to the hard work of suffragettes and the contribution of women to the war effort at home and abroad. The Calgary Eye Opener, *18 Mar 1916* **Right.** *Long live the French Canadians. [tr.] In mid-September of 1916 Canadian troops were fighting the Battle of the Somme in France. The 22nd battalion from Quebec (the Vandoos) were among the Canadians who reached and held their objective. An English Canadian cartoonist celebrates their achievement.* The Brantford Expositor, *25 Sep 1916*

BILINGUALISM

When Franco-Ontarians complained about Ontario's language laws to the Liberal opposition in Ontario, or to the Conservative government in Ottawa, they received little support. Politicians did not want to antagonize English voters in Ontario. The issue badly divided English and French Canadians (the bulldog and the poodle). Saturday Night, *Toronto, 20 May 1916*

LA CAUSE
Que le nationaliste et le fanatique laissent les deux chiens tranquille et ils feront bon ménage.

THE CAUSE. Let the nationalist and the fanatic leave the two dogs alone and they will get along together. [tr.] The Ontario government's decision to restrict the linguistic rights of the French-speaking minority resulted in a bitter dispute. Statements made by extremists on both sides helped prepare the way for the coming heated debate on conscription. Le Canard, *Montreal, 6 Aug 1916*

BORDEN: Ontario ne veut plus fournir de soldats. **JOHN BULL**: Emmenez les moutons de Québec.

Left. *BORDEN: Ontario does not want to supply any more soldiers. JOHN BULL: Bring on the sheep from Quebec. [tr.] In the spring of 1916 there was a serious decline in enlistment in the Canadian army. The need for workers on farms and in factories had eliminated unemployment, and high casualty rates overseas discouraged volunteers. John Bull (Britain) suggests, ironically, that Prime Minister Borden should seek reinforcements from Quebec. Le Canard, Montreal, 23 July 1916*
Right. *Many Canadians resented the fact that the United States was profiting from the war while Canadians paid heavily in lives and wealth for what they considered a just cause. The Toronto Daily News, 12 Dec 1916*

WOE IS ME
Yesterday I was too proud to fight. Today I am too fat to fight.

CHEZ LES BOCHES

SERVICE NATIONAL
Impression de l'assemblée du Monument National.

Left. *Feeling threatened by the growing number of Francophones moving to the province, the Ontario government passed Regulation 17 which restricted French instruction. A Quebec cartoonist compares the restrictions with the German treatment of minorities in Europe.* Le Nationaliste, *Montreal, 20 Feb 1916*
Right. NATIONAL SERVICE. *Impression of the assembly at the Monument National [tr.] In a speech at the Monument National in Montreal, Prime Minister Borden appealed to the public to support a plan to allocate manpower to the war effort at home and abroad. The cartoonist suggests that the National Service would ultimately provide cannon fodder for the European war. The cartoon was removed by the censor from* La Bataille, *Montreal, 14 Dec 1916.*

THE REAL WINNER IN EUROPE   **NO BELIEVER IN SIGNS**

Left. *This cartoon is one of the few anti-war cartoons published in Canada during the First World War.* The Nutcracker, *Calgary, 16 Mar 1917* **Right.** *In April 1917 four Canadian divisions fought together for the first time at Vimy Ridge in northwestern France. Their victory was a turning point for Allied forces in the war and a turning point in Canada's passage from colony to nation. The battle helped unite the Canadian army in France and public opinion at home.* The Vancouver Daily Province, *12 Apr 1917*

TIME FOR A HOG-KILLING!
THE HOG: I tell you, Sir Robert, you're giving us a great government. Business was never so good in my line.

Inflation was a serious problem during the First World War. The high demand for food in Europe drove up prices. In response the government set up a Board of Grain Supervisors to regulate the grain trade. This cartoon suggests that the board will look after the interests of business, not the public. Soldiers' families, who were on fixed incomes, were particularly hard hit by the increases. The Vancouver Daily Sun, *23 July 1917*

REDUCING WILL DO HIM GOOD

Once the government decided to conscript manpower, pressure mounted for the government to conscript wealth as well. Finance minister W. T. White introduced the Business Profits Tax in 1916 and an Income War Tax in 1917. The Grain Growers' Guide, *Winnipeg, 1 Aug 1917*

A POOR BUSINESS PROPOSITION

ROYAL COMMISSION: "Now, John, I'd like to see you buy these two small pigs. True they're poor and mean and scrawny and the price is high and you'll lose money on them, but you ought to buy them." **JOHN CANADA**: "Not much. I'll take all three or none."

The overexpansion of Canada's railway system meant that the government had to provide railways such as the Grand Trunk Pacific and the Canadian Northern Railway with substantial aid. Some people suggested that the railway system be nationalized. The Grain Growers' Guide, *Winnipeg, 9 May 1917*

BORDEN ET SON ÂNE

LES PURS
Of course we don't want conscription.
But we'll let Quebec do the kicking.

Left. BORDEN AND HIS DONKEY. By 1917 voluntary enlistment in the Canadian army was well below the casualty rate. After a trip to England and the front lines Prime Minister Borden returned to Canada convinced that conscription was necessary. Opposition to the idea was particularly strong in Quebec. Le Soleil, Quebec, 26 May 1917 Right. THE PURE. Many people in English Canada also opposed conscription. La Conscription, July 1917

FOURNISSEURS, PROFITEURS & EXPLOITEURS

Ceux que les guerres n'ont jamais empêché de prospérer: "Il y a 30,000 millionnaires nouveaux aux États-Unis, depuis la guerre." *New York Journal*

Left. SUPPLIERS, PROFITEERS & EXPLOITERS. *The wars have never prevented them from prospering: "There are 30,000 new millionaires in the United States since the beginning of the war." [tr.] The Quebec artist was embittered by the fact that so many businessmen continued to prosper from the war at the expense of those sent to fight in it.* Le Nationaliste, *Montreal, 23 Sep 1917* **Right.** THE PLOT. *Are the people ready to let themselves be crushed and wrung for the profit of unionist exploiters? [tr.] In order to ensure his election Conservative prime minister Borden decided to form a coalition government of Conservatives and Liberals. This cartoon questions his motives.* Le Canada, *Montreal, 6 Dec 1917*

LE COMPLOT

Le peuple est-il pret à se laisser tordre et broyer pour le profit des exploiteurs unionists?

HIS IDEA OF FIGHTING A FIRE

WHY WORRY? THE FIGHT IS IN FRANCE

Left. Opposition leader Laurier opposed the idea of a coalition government and proposed that the government hold a referendum on the issue of conscription. Most English Canadian Liberals supported Borden and a Union government was formed in October 1917. The Toronto World, 8 Nov 1917 **Right.** This British Columbia cartoon is highly critical of pacifists, Quebeckers and Liberal politicians (such as McInnis) who refused to join the Union government and give unqualified support to the Canadian army, which was involved in a life and death struggle with Germany. The Vancouver World, 7 Dec 1917

FOLLOW THE WHITE PLUME

MOTHERS, WIVES, SISTERS, LOVERS
A loyal Government has placed a weapon in your hand to defend yourselves against the murdering burglar who would treat you as he has treated your Belgian sisters. Make good use of it by supporting that Government.

Left. Government election propaganda claimed that a vote for Laurier was a vote for the Kaiser and against the soldiers in the trenches. Nearly all of the major newspapers supported the Union government. The Evening Telegram, *Toronto, 20 Nov 1917* **Right.** *In order to make sure that his government won the December election, Borden made drastic changes to the franchise, and gave the vote to wives, mothers and sisters of soldiers overseas. The cartoonist directs the women to use their vote to elect the Union government, which would guarantee conscription.* The Brantford Expositor, *8 Dec 1917*

LES DEUX DRAPEAUX
CATHERINE: Quel drapeau suivre?
BAPTISTE: Y a pas à hésiter. Vive le Canada! Vive Laurier!

Left. CATHERINE: *Which flag should we follow?* BAPTISTE: *No need to hesitate. Long live Canada! Long live Laurier!* [tr.] *Led by men such as Henri Bourassa, many people in Quebec saw the election as a struggle between those who placed Britain's interests first and those who placed Canada's interests first.* La Presse, *Montreal, 14 Dec 1917* **Right.** *As election day approached, the Liberal and Conservative newspapers that supported the Union government became stronger in their patriotic fervour and anti-Laurier sentiment. Laurier was portrayed as a supporter of the Kaiser and even of the Bolsheviks. Liberal supporters in Ontario published their own newspaper and struck back with cartoons such as this one.* The Grit, *Toronto, 12 Dec 1917*

THE DEVIL'S BREW

**THE FAULT, DEAR BRUTUS, LIES WITH OURSELVES,
NOT WITH OUR STARS**

OVER THE HEADS OF THE POLITICIANS

Left. The Wartime Election Act was designed to manipulate the franchise to ensure Borden's re-election. This cartoon portrays the Act and Borden's Union government as a nest of cobras. The City of Vancouver Archives, 1917. *Right.* For many Anglophone voters the election and the issue of conscription became a test of loyalty to the troops at the front. The Vancouver Daily Province, *15 Dec 1917.*

DEEDS, NOT WORDS
Thanks Samuel! Your heart is as big as your country is broad.
You have Canada's heart-felt gratitude.

CHRISTMAS 1917

Left. On December 6, 1917, two ships collided in Halifax harbour. A munitions ship loaded with 6,400 tons of explosives and ammunition blew up. Over 1600 people were killed in one of the worst disasters in Canadian history. The Americans were among the first to send relief to Halifax. The Montreal Daily Star, 14 Dec 1917 Right. This cartoon contrasts the wealth enjoyed by politicians and businessmen during the war with the relative poverty of soldiers' families. The Canadian Liberal Monthly, Ottawa, Dec 1917

EVOLUTION

SIGNS OF THE TIMES
John Buli alters the sign again.

Left. This cartoon focuses on the positive results of the war, which led to an expansion of agriculture and industry and helped promote a sense of Canadian identity. The Montreal Daily Star, 1918 ***Right.*** *The British government rewarded the Dominion premiers for their war effort by inviting them to London in 1917 to sit as members of an Imperial War Cabinet. The Dominions were referred to in a resolution as "autonomous nations of an Imperial Commonwealth." The resolution reflected the growing conviction that they should attain national status.* The Halifax Herald, 3 Aug 1918

IT SHALL NOT BE

THE GOOD KNIGHT

Left. *Veterans, whose wives and children lived on meagre pay during the war, felt that they were entitled to a just financial settlement and resented the fact that others had profited from the war at their expense.* The B.C. Veterans Weekly, *Vancouver, 23 May 1918* ***Right.*** *Many Canadians objected to Britain giving, and selling, special honours to citizens who became wealthy during the war, while those who served in the military were not so honoured. The practice ended in Canada after a baronetcy was given to a businessman whose company had made huge profits selling pork.* Saturday Night, *Toronto, 23 Feb 1918*

THE SILENT WITNESS

ABOMB(INABLE) ATTACK

Left. Two weeks before the December 1917 election the Union government promised to exempt farmers' sons from conscription. This pledge succeeded in weakening support for the Liberals in rural areas. When heavy casualties in the spring forced Borden to cancel his promise, the farmers marched to Ottawa in an unsuccessful attempt to get him to change his mind. The Grain Growers' Guide, *Winnipeg, 22 May 1918* **Right.** *In March 1918 Borden extended voting rights to all women in Canada aged twenty-one and over. British Columbia artist Emily Carr summarizes many of the issues she hoped would receive more attention once women had the vote.* Western Woman's Weekly, *Vancouver, 7 Feb 1918*

I SHALL NEVER PERMIT MY POOR, DELICATE BABY TO BE ROBBED OF HIS BOTTLE. NEVER! NEVER! NEVER!

HE MUST BE WEANED

Left. In 1919 there were over a quarter of a million motor vehicles in Canada. The automobile changed the lives of Canadians and challenged city and provincial governments to improve roads and regulate drivers. The Halifax Herald, *1 Nov 1919* **Right.** *Canadian industries had grown and prospered during the war. Tariffs had been necessary to protect growing industries from competition, but once those industries were strong enough to compete the tariffs were to be removed. This Western Canadian cartoon argues that the time had come to do so.* The Grain Growers' Guide, Winnipeg, *5 Feb 1919*

IL FAUT SOULAGER L'HUMANITÉ SOUFFRANTE
La Prohibition n'existe pas pour ceux qui se disent malades.

WE MUST RELIEVE SUFFERING HUMANITY. Prohibition does not exist for those who claim to be ill. [tr.] Prohibition was very difficult to enforce. Brewers and distillers continued to make liquor for export, hotel saloons sold something called "near beer," bootlegging became popular, and doctors issued prescriptions for "medicinal" alcohol. Le Canada, Montreal, 18 May 1919

QUAND LE VIN ET LA BIÈRE SERONT DISPARUS
Au Café
Garçon: Cocaïne ou morphine?

THE NEXT STEP

Left. *WHEN THE WINE AND BEER HAVE DISAPPEARED. Waiter: Cocaine or morphine? [tr.] A Quebec cartoonist suggests that if alcoholic beverages are no longer available people will turn to other, stronger drugs.* La Presse, *Montreal, 9 Apr 1919* ***Right.*** *Inspired by their success in bringing about prohibition ("slaying the demon rum"), some moral reformers were ready to slay the demon tobacco.* Saturday Night, *Toronto, 28 June 1919*

GIVE THE POOR BABY A CHANCE!
The odds he is up against must be reduced.

SAFETY FIRST
MADAME MONTREAL: Dear me! I think the dog had better be unchained.

Left. *Governments were slow to set up legislation to ensure a pure milk supply. Contaminated milk was a significant cause of infant mortality until tuberculin testing of dairy herds, sanitary collection and delivery of milk, pasteurization and rigorous inspection were enforced.* The Montreal Daily Star, *4 Oct 1919*
Right. *The Spanish flu was introduced to Canada by troops returning from the war. In 1918–1919 it spread throughout Canada and killed about 50,000 people. The epidemic ultimately led to the establishment of the federal Department of Health.* The Montreal Daily Star, *21 Jan 1919*

WATCH THEM COME!
The greatest magnet in the world today

WHAT HE REALLY WANTS

Left. Although Canada faced problems adjusting from a wartime to a peacetime economy, the country was rich in natural resources. The cartoonist predicts that immigrants from Europe will once again be attracted by Canada's great potential. The Montreal Daily Star, *18 Aug 1919* **Right.** *Returned soldiers were swamped with praise from politicians and the press, but what they really wanted were jobs. A sluggish postwar economy and the vast number of men involved made it impossible to meet their needs. Veterans had to campaign to get the government to pay them an allowance.* The Halifax Herald, *15 Feb 1919*

LE COÛT DE LA VIE NE VEUT PLUS DESCENDRE
L'OUVRIER: On a vu la "fin" de la guerre, mais quand verrons-nous la "fin" de la "faim"?

THE COST OF LIVING IS NOT GOING TO GO DOWN. THE WORKER: We've seen the end of the war, but when are we going to see the end of hunger? [tr.] Many workers suffered a decline in their standard of living during the war. Wages had not kept up with the increased cost of living. The large number of returning soldiers entering the job market resulted in increased unemployment and made it difficult for workers to improve their lot. Le Canard, Montreal, 25 Jan 1919

A WILD CRY TO ORGANIZED LABOR AND THE RETURNED SOLDIERS TO COME TO THE HELP OF SPECIAL PRIVILEGE

The Canadian Reconstruction Association issued a leaflet in 1919 urging returned soldiers and organized labour to ignore the efforts of the Grain Growers to organize them into a third political force. This cartoon ridicules the Association's claim that the Bolsheviks were behind the farmers' movement. The Grain Growers' Guide, *Winnipeg, 16 Apr 1919*

LEGISLATIVE INSECTICIDE BADLY NEEDED
The destructive worms at the roots of Canada's Reconstruction garden.

Left. *On May 15, 1919, most of the workers in Winnipeg decided to stage a general strike to support demands for union recognition and higher wages. Business and government opposed the strike because their interests were threatened and they felt that the strike leaders were foreign radicals who wanted to destroy capitalism.* The Brantford Expositor, *9 June 1919* **Right.** *From the workers' point of view the issues involved in the Winnipeg General Strike were simple: the right of collective bargaining and an increase in wages. They felt themselves to be unfairly attacked by wealthy businessmen backed by the government and the police.* The British Columbia Federationist, *Vancouver, 13 Jun 1919*

READY FOR ALL THAT MIGHT HAPPEN.　　　　　**"JUSTICE IN WINNIPEG!"**

Left. *The government and the business community recruited returned soldiers to oppose a general strike in Winnipeg. The government feared that radicals were behind the strike and might provoke a revolution like the recent Bolshevik uprising in Russia. Some veterans supported the government but most sided with the unions.* The Manitoba Veteran, *7 June 1919* **Right.** *On June 17 the government ordered the arrest of ten strike leaders on charges of sedition. A few days later a group of demonstrators, strikers and returned soldiers was charged by police on horseback. The strike ended on June 20.* The Alberta Non-Partisan, Calgary, *7 July 1919*

DON'T BE SILLY!

Man in middle (who pays for it all): Here, get together! Make a team of your horses and let us get somewhere!

Labour–management conflict did not end with the collapse of the Winnipeg General Strike. Western Canadians founded the One Big Union (OBU) to fight for increased wages and improved working conditions. Employers wanted to roll back the gains that unions had won during the war. The average Canadian was caught in the middle of the struggle between capital and labour. The Brantford Expositor, *18 Sep 1919*

The One Big Union wanted all workers to join industry-wide unions and use the general strike to cripple the economy and force concessions. Such radical tactics were equated with bolshevism. Canadian Labor Press, *15 Nov 1919*

The System of Partyism, and What the Farmers Got Out Of It

A Better System, and What Special Privilege & Co. Will Get Out Of It

Farmers felt that the Liberal and Conservative parties were not paying enough attention to such rural problems as the high cost of living, the cost of farm machinery, excessive freight rates and rural depopulation. They deserted the old parties and formed new provincial and federal parties. The United Farmers of Ontario were elected in October and the National Progressive Party was established at the federal level. The Grain Growers' Guide, *Winnipeg, 26 Nov 1919*

HEY DIDDLE DIDDLE — THE MAN IN THE MIDDLE

The high cost of living was often blamed on special interests. The Grain Growers' Guide, *Winnipeg, 8 Sep 1920*

A TRUE BALANCE

"A fair day's work for a fair day's pay" became the rallying cry of union organizers. Workers would gladly have settled for the ideal portrayed in this cartoon. In the 1920s most settled for far less. Working conditions were unsafe, living conditions were poor and wages were so low that it was difficult to avoid poverty. The Labor Leader, *Toronto, 3 Dec 1920*

SHE MAKES HIM PAY FOR IT TOO!
Is it not high time to break away from her apron strings?

WANTED, A LULLABY!
Plain Honest Mr. Workingman begins to wonder if the pesky brats of discord, which make of life a nightmare, will ever be put to sleep.

Left. Many people suggested that Canadians should purchase locally manufactured goods. The increased economic activity would reduce unemployment and strengthen Canadian independence. The Montreal Daily Star, *16 Feb 1920* **Right.** *Labour was badly divided in the early 1920s. Some groups, including the One Big Union and the Industrial Workers of the World, wanted to destroy capitalism. More moderate groups wanted unions to fight for improved working and living conditions within the current economic system.* The Labor Leader, *Toronto, 14 May 1920*

SHALL *THESE* BE THE ARBITERS OF CANADA'S FUTURE?

OUR BARGAIN SALE

Left. *In 1920 Canada was admitted to the League of Nations. Canadians resented the fact that so many small Latin American republics were given equal status. The "Monroe Doctrine" refers to the long-standing "hands off the Americas" policy of the United States and suggests that those countries will favour the US at the expense of Canada.* The Halifax Herald, *18 Feb 1920* **Right.** *The British Columbia economy declined badly after the war and did not start to recover until 1922. The BC government offers investment opportunities to business interests while an overtaxed citizen and a returned veteran look on.* The Western Idea, Vancouver, *13 Aug 1920*

THE QUESTION OF THE DAY

In the Prairie provinces everyone depended on the success of agriculture. This Western Canadian cartoon hints at the political and economic power of the farmer.
The Grain Growers' Guide, *Winnipeg, 7 July 1920*

HORRIBLE REVENGE

Quebec is having its—"hour."

DIVIDING THE SPOILS

Left. *Quebec was the last province to feel the effects of prohibition and the first province to abandon it. Wine and beer reappeared in Quebec in 1919 and the province soon experienced an increase in tourism.* The Montreal Daily Star, *5 Mar 1920* **Right.** *After the war most people realized that prohibition was not working, but did not want to return to the days of uncontrolled drinking. British Columbia pioneered the controlled sale of liquor in government stores. This prohibitionist cartoon suggests that the government's motive was economic.* The Vancouver Sun, *19 Oct 1920*

NO MATTER WHO SUFFERS
Barleycorn Trying hard to save John.

This cartoon, opposing the end of prohibition, attacks the arguments of those who felt that people should have the freedom to decide for themselves if they want to drink. The Farmer's Sun, *Toronto, 13 Apr 1921*

PALS

ONE SIGN OF RETURNING WORLD SANITY

Left. *Support for gun control is not a new phenomenon.* The Montreal Daily Star, *26 Jan 1921* **Right.** *Jazz became very popular during the war and in the years that followed. Conservative groups blamed it for a decline in morality among young people. The cartoonist uses an African stereotype popular at the time to mock the origins of jazz.* The Montreal Daily Star, *11 Feb 1921*

Left. WHAT WILL HAPPEN? *If the Canadiens continue to desert while immigrants arrive by the boatload and the Americans pursue their conquests... This is what will happen: here lies the faith of Brébeuf; here lies the race of Champlain; here lies the language of Dollard. [tr.]* **Upper right.** DEMAND RESPECT FOR FRENCH *... on the signs of your merchants... in the theatres and cinemas... on food products... [tr.]* **Lower right.** WRONGS TO REMEDY. *Commercial travellers [postage stamps] visit the whole world in the name of Canada yet speak only one language, English. [tr.] These cartoons appeared in a periodical promoting French language and culture.* Almanach de la Langue Française, *Montreal, 1921 and 1922.*

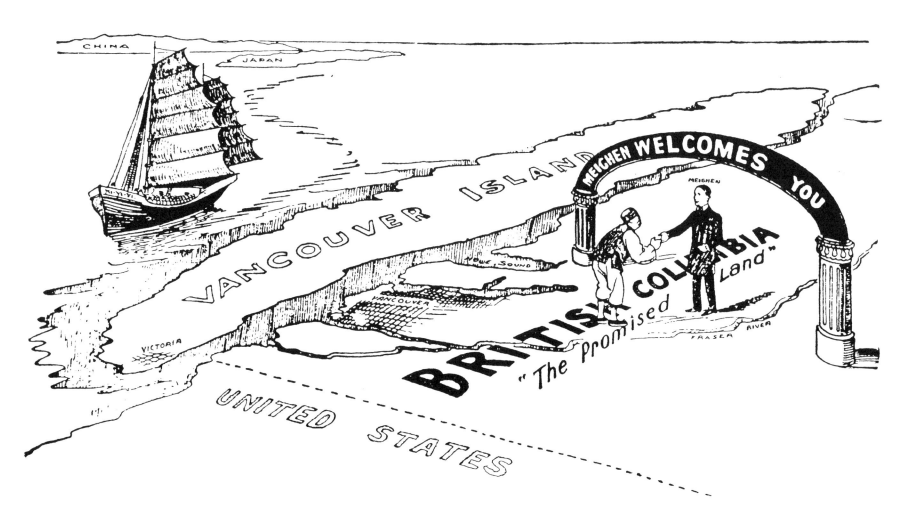

LIBERAL CANDIDATES ARE PLEDGED TO A WHITE BRITISH COLUMBIA

Immigration from Asia was a hot political issue in British Columbia in the federal election of 1921. This cartoon from a Liberal campaign ad draws attention to the Conservative policy of increased immigration. The Vancouver Sun, *4 Dec 1921*

BRITISH COLUMBIA HATES THE CHINKS, JAPS AND MORMONS

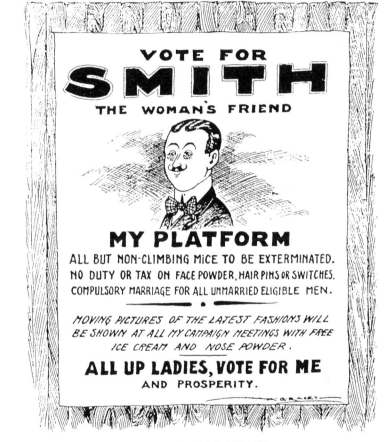

HINT TO POLITICIANS
How to secure the woman's vote.
"The coming general elections are the first in which women's votes are a factor, one million and a quarter women voters being added to the list."

Left. As unemployment rose and wages fell in British Columbia after the war, returned veterans and trade unions called for an end to immigration from Asia. In 1923 the King government would replace the head tax with a law which virtually excluded Chinese immigration, and Canada and Japan would agreed to limit Japanese immigration to about 150 individuals a year. Mormons, who favored polygamy, were also unwelcome. The cartoon reflects the prejudices of many people at the time. The Veteran, *Toronto, July 1921* **Right.** *The 1921 election was the first one in which all women were eligible to vote on the same basis as men.* The Montreal Daily Star, *7 Sep 1921*

WHY CANADIAN FARMERS ARE IN POLITICS
1885   1921

LE ROI S'AMUSE

Left. The 1921 census showed that the urban population equalled the rural population for the first time in Canadian history. Farmers were worried that they would lose their political power and influence to the cities, and became politically active. The Vancouver Sun, 11 Sep 1921 **Right.** THE KING AMUSES HIMSELF. *In the federal election of 1921 Liberal leader King tried to balance the desire of Western Canada for low tariffs with that of Quebec for high tariffs. The Evening Telegram, Toronto, 3 Oct 1921*

Can you realize the utter helplessness and awful hopelessness of the plight in which the families of thousands of unemployed find themselves? **NO WORK, NO MONEY** and **NO FOOD**. With everything gone for the purchase of food to stave off the Wolf of Hunger, the situation has become desperate, so desperate that the aid of citizens more fortunately placed is invoked. What will **YOU** do? The cry of the hungry little ones must be heard. So your aid is asked. Can **YOU**, will **YOU** refuse?

The postwar economic boom came to a sudden end. In 1921 unemployment was well over 15 percent. Jobless workers and their families had to depend on private charities for the basics of food, clothing and shelter. Many suffered great hardship. One Big Union Bulletin, *Winnipeg, 25 June 1921*

Political Slogans Illustrated: "PROTECTION CREATES WORK" (For the Politicians)

Conservative prime minister Meighen had the misfortune to replace Borden just before the beginning of a postwar depression. As unemployment increased and wages fell, Meighen had little to offer Canadians but a promise to protect industries by keeping tariffs high. The Grain Growers' Guide, *Winnipeg, 16 Nov 1921*

THE VESTED INTERESTS: "MEIGHEN WILL LEAD US THROUGH"

Farmers and labourers were disenchanted with the old parties and many supported the Progressive Party. In the coming federal election Meighen would fail to obtain a majority and King would need the support of the Progressives in order to govern. The Citizen, Ottawa, 3 Dec 1921

CANADA HAS AT LEAST ONE THRIVING BUSINESS

WHY BOYS LEAVE HOME AND GO TO VARSITY

Left. *The Civil Service Act of 1918, passed by the Union government of Robert Borden, did much to lessen political patronage at the federal level and establish a merit system in the civil service. However, patronage still flourished at the municipal and provincial levels. Public servants who supported the losing party in an election were replaced by supporters of the winning party.* The Halifax Herald, *10 June 1922* **Right.** *After the First World War more and more young women were attending university, apparently distracting some young men from their studies.* The Goblin, *Toronto, Mar 1922*

CHASSONS LES HYPOCRITES DE LA "LORD'S DAY ALLIANCE"

BAPTISTE: Mon v'limeux, tu veux faire du dimanche un cimetière? Tu veux tout fermer, nous empêcher de fumer, rire, lire, manger, et... d'aimer, le dimanche? Eh! bien, tiens; attrappe ça pour te fermer la g...le.

LET'S GET RID OF THE LORD'S DAY ALLIANCE HYPOCRITES. BAPTISTE: You hypocrites, do you want to turn Sunday into a cemetery? You want to close everything, stop us from smoking, reading, laughing, eating and... loving on Sundays? Well then, here's something to shut you up. [tr.] In 1906 the federal government passed the Lord's Day Act, which gave the provinces the power to restrict trade, labour and recreation on Sunday. The strongest opposition to the Act came from Quebec, where many saw it as a Protestant attack on Catholicism. Le Canard, *Montreal, 5 Mar 1922*

LA PROHIBITION EST-ELLE LA CAUSE DU FLÉAU DE LA "DROGUE"?

LA MORT: Puisque les gouvernements veulent prendre le contrôle des boissons, je me réserve le droit de la "Commission des Drogues."

IS PROHIBITION THE CAUSE OF THE CURSE OF "DRUGS" ? DEATH: Since the governments want to take control of beverages, I reserve for myself the right of the "Drug Commission." [tr.] Drugs were a growing problem in Montreal in the 1920s. The cartoonist blames the situation on government restrictions on the sale of alcohol. Le Canard, *Toronto, 15 Oct 1922*

WHY TORONTO IS DISLIKED
The Fat Grows Fatter; The Lean Leaner

As a new source of light and power, hydroelectricity had a huge impact on Ontario's economy. A publicly owned power system under Adam Beck expanded rapidly. The electrification of rural areas did not begin in earnest until 1921, when the province began subsidizing the construction of rural transmission lines. The Farmers' Sun, *Toronto, 4 Feb 1922*

SAVE THE RUSSIAN CHILDREN
With Every Meal Comes the Thought.

After nearly four years of revolution and civil war the economy of the USSR was close to collapse. Canada, which had a grain surplus, was asked to send food to prevent Russian children from starving. The Farmers' Sun, *Toronto, 9 May 1922*

IT'S UP TO SOMEBODY

NOVA SCOTIA'S HANDICAP

Left. The hereditary council of the Six Nations near Brantford, Ontario, felt threatened by the federal government's efforts to weaken their authority and speed up the process of assimilation. In May 1922 they launched a vigorous protest against the perceived threat and renewed their struggle to affirm their ancient right of self-government. The Globe, Toronto, 12 May 1922 ***Right.*** *The postwar Depression started in the Maritimes in 1920. The advantageous freight rates previously enjoyed by the Maritimes were lost between 1918 and 1922 as the Intercolonial Railway was absorbed by the Canadian National Railway system. High freight rates favoured Toronto, Montreal and even Liverpool, England, in trade with Western Canada.* The Halifax Herald, 20 Jan 1922

THE NOVA SCOTIAN MINER
AS REPRESENTED BY THE INTERESTS AND AS HE REALLY IS

After the war the coal industry in Nova Scotia had to compete with the overproduction of coal in the United States and the growing popularity of hydroelectric power and oil in Central Canada. When the miners attempted to fight wage cuts and improve their working conditions they were portrayed as radical militants. The Halifax Herald, *25 Aug 1922*

WITH A SLIGHT ALTERATION
Why not leave the Harp on the Royal Arms?

THAT PERSISTENT CALLER

Left. *Borden wanted the Dominions to have a voice in the foreign policy of the British Empire and proposed that they consult on all important matters of common concern. Differences among the Dominions at the Imperial Conference of 1921 showed the difficulties involved.* The Montreal Daily Star, *9 Jan 1922*
Right. *In 1922 Turkey threatened British troops occupying the strategic straits separating the Mediterranean and the Black Seas. Prime Minister King made it clear that Canada would not aid England if war broke out. The Chanak crisis marked an important step on the road to an independent foreign policy for Canada.* The Halifax Herald, *19 Sep 1922*

HEADS AND TAILS

UNCLE SAM: "What I cut off goes to you, Johnnie Canuck,
and what's left belongs to me."

CANADA AND THE NAVY
His Proud Position.

Left. In 1923 Canada negotiated and signed a fishing treaty with the United States without any British involvement. The Halibut Treaty marked another step in establishing Canada's status as an independent nation. The cartoonist suggests that the results were less than ideal. The Evening Telegram, *Toronto, 19 Mar 1923*
Right. The King government severely reduced Canada's armed forces. The Montreal Daily Star, *18 May 1922.*

TRIUMPH OF WHITE OVER BLACK
A Dream That Could Be Made Come True.

CANADA, ACCORDING TO AMERICAN MOVIES

Left. The harnessing of hydroelectric power and the development of long-distance transmission lines in the early 1900s launched Canada into the age of electric power and lessened her dependence on King Coal, seen with his crown knocked off and sceptre broken. The Montreal Daily Star, *24 Nov 1923*
Right. According to American movies of the early 1920s "the whole population of Canada, from Halifax to Vancouver, over fifty in number," gathers in a dance hall every evening "to gamble, fight, dance, plan bank robberies and to drink neat whiskey out of diminutive glasses such as are seen only in the U.S.A." The Montreal Daily Star, *28 Nov 1923*

OUTGROWN THEIR CLOTHES

The visit to the tailor, or, the youngsters' rapid growth necessitates new outfitting.

DOESN'T GET THE BIG ONES

Left. The 1921 census confirmed the growth of the Western Canadian provinces. The redistribution of seats in Parliament strengthened the West and weakened the Maritimes. The Montreal Daily Star, 15 Feb 1923 Right. Before the independent Civil Service Commission was established in 1917 political appointments were based almost exclusively on party loyalty. Patronage and merit co-existed until the 1940s, when the forces opposed to patronage won. The Halifax Herald, 24 Feb 1923

IN ONE END — OUT ANOTHER

JACK CANUCK: "Holding the bag is about all I seem to be getting out of this!"

THE WEDGE

Left. Emigration to the United States was a serious problem during the 1920s. Nearly a million people left Canada for better opportunities. Many immigrants used Canada as a portal to the United States, which restricted immigration from Europe but not from Canada. The Halifax Herald, *10 Apr 1923* **Right.** *The cartoonist suggests that the Roman Catholic Church was undermining Canada through its demands for special privileges.* The Sentinel and Orange and Protestant Advocate, *Toronto, 4 Dec 1923*

IF EVENTUALLY, WHY NOT NOW?

A strike by steelworkers for union recognition in Sydney, Nova Scotia, was met by provincial police and a bloody riot. Coal miners went out to support the steelworkers, and bitter unrest continued for another two years. In 1937 the province would become the first to legislate union recognition and compulsory bargaining. The Halifax Herald, *12 June 1923*

"INFLUENCE"   "BRIBERY"

A DISTINCTION IN TERMS BUT NOT IN PURPOSE

A Western cartoonist suggests that the banks, railways and large industries purchased the support of the Liberal and Conservative parties and public officials.
Westerners felt that their demands for such things as lower tariffs, better freight rates, control of their natural resources and a railway to Hudson's Bay were blocked
by these interests. The Grain Growers' Guide, *Winnipeg, 7 May 1924*

BEWARE!

LOVER OF CLEAN SPORT: You'll follow him if you fail to conform to the standards of decency on the ice.

L'OUEST A UN SOLIDE APPÉTIT!

KING: Quatre portefeuilles? Mais t'es pas sérieux, mon vieux. Je ne les ai pas! Et où veux-tu que je les prenne? **CRERAR**: Dans le panier de la vieille...

Left. In the early 1900s lacrosse was considered the national game. As its popularity declined, interest in hockey grew. The cartoonist suggests that violent play had much to do with the decline of lacrosse and might destroy hockey as well. The Montreal Daily Star, 3 Mar 1924 ***Right.** THE WEST IS HUNGRY. KING: Four portfolios? You're not serious, old fellow. I don't have them! And where do you expect me to get them? CRERAR: From the old lady's basket... [tr.] In the federal election of 1921 the Prairie provinces elected 38 Progressives and three Liberals; Quebec had voted solid Liberal. Athough King needed the support of the Progressives to stay in power, he did not want to undermine his power base in Quebec and rejected Crerar's demands.* La Patrie, Montreal, 10 Jan 1924

APRÈS LE DISCOURS SUR LE BUDGET CANADIEN
Le coup de pioche dans le mur tarifaire.

LA MARIONETTE

Left. AFTER THE CANADIAN BUDGET SPEECH. *Pickaxe attack on the tariff wall. [tr.] A few by-election losses eliminated Prime Minister King's slender majority in Parliament. In a successful attempt to secure the votes of Western Progressives, King reduced or abolished tariffs on equipment such as farm implements used in primary industries. The cartoonist blames his action for the loss of jobs in Canadian manufacturing and the emigration of more workers to the United States.* La Patrie, *Montreal, 12 Apr 1924* **Right.** THE PUPPET. *Progressive party leader Robert Forke was quick to take credit for the lower tariff on farm implements passed by King's government.* La Patrie, *Montreal, 10 May 1924*

LUMBERING IN CANADA

CE QUI POURRAIT ARRIVER

Left. A Montreal cartoonist suggests that Canadians should place an embargo on the export of raw logs to the United States, where they were used to make pulp and paper in American mills. The Montreal Daily Star, 20 Mar 1924 **Right.** WHAT COULD HAPPEN. FATHER: It used to be a forest. [tr.] A Montreal cartoonist expresses concern over the clear-cutting of Quebec's forests. La Presse, Montreal, 26 July 1924

WHAT THE UNEASY PUBLIC WISH TO KNOW
Is police protection being afforded for this state of affairs, or is it not?

MR. VANCOUVER: These things certainly are a nuisance. I wish I knew (ahem!) where they are coming from.

Left. Police tolerance of prostitution was a matter of concern for the citizens of Montreal. **The Montreal Daily Star,** *18 Sep 1924* **Right.** *Gambling had been prohibited in Canada in 1917 as the government sought to concentrate all efforts and finances on the war effort. After the war betting was once again allowed. Gambling at the racetrack was seen as the cause of many criminal activities.* **The British Columbia Monthly,** *Vancouver, Sep 1924*

THE PRECOCIOUS BOY, OR WHAT WILL HE BE UP TO NEXT?
THE BOY'S DAD: See here, young fellow, this Wild West high-handed little game you're playing's got to stop. Yer getting me in wrong with the neighbors as well as the family...

OUR HOSPITAL PROBLEM
As these institutions are for the benefit of the general public, why should not the general public lend a hand in carrying the load?

*Left. Chicago created an international problem when it illegally diverted water from Lake Michigan into the Ohio River drainage basin. The diversion affected the levels of the Great Lakes and power production on the St. Lawrence River. The Montreal Daily Star, 7 Jan 1925 **Right**. Most general hospitals at this time relied on donations. They were devoted primarily to treating the poor, as wealthier citizens preferred to be treated at home. As equipment became more sophisticated and personnel better trained, more people used hospitals, and taxation to support them became necessary. The Montreal Daily Star, 27 Nov 1925*

THE MARCH ON OTTAWA

Lobbyists for all sorts of groups descended on Ottawa for the 1925 session of Parliament, the last before an expected election. The government had to try to balance the demands of different regions and interests in dealing with freight rates, tariffs, the cost of living and control of financial institutions. The Grain Growers' Guide, *Winnipeg, 28 Feb 1925*

THAT'S THE SPIRIT

The Maritimes voted Liberal in 1921 but King's minority government had to court the Western Progressives to stay in power. The Maritimers retaliated by voting Conservative in 1925 and championed their grievances under a movement known as Maritime Rights. The movement managed to improve freight rates, the ports of Saint John and Halifax, and transportation to Prince Edward Island. The Halifax Herald, *18 Apr 1925*

CANADA UNDER THE STARS AND STRIPES?
"Why Girls Leave Home"

DAD LETS SON DRIVE

Left. The British government spent much of its time and effort on European affairs. British interest in Canada declined in the interwar period and American interest increased. The Daily Express, *London, England, Mar 1925* **Right.** *The cartoon suggests that in 1925 independence for the Dominions was an illusion. The "son" may hold the reins but "dad" has the controlling grip.* The Toronto Daily Star, *17 June 1925*

DANGER!
Look out for the undertow.

In the 1920s American investment in Canada exceeded British investment and grew rapidly thereafter. Canada was also flooded with American films and magazines. The emigration of hundreds of thousands of Canadians to the United States strengthened these connections. The Montreal Daily Star, *8 July 1925*

CANADA'S PROPOSED NEW FLAG — A SUGGESTION TO THE PRESENT ADMINISTRATION AT OTTAWA
This design is offered to the Flag Committee free of charge. The black background represents the future of the Dominion at the present rate of national debt increase. The balance of the design needs no explanation.

The design for the flag reflects the high level of British and American investment in Canada and the rising debt of the Canadian National Railway, portrayed as a costly white elephant. Business interests in Montreal particularly disliked the idea of a state-owned railway. The Montreal Daily Star, *11 June 1925*

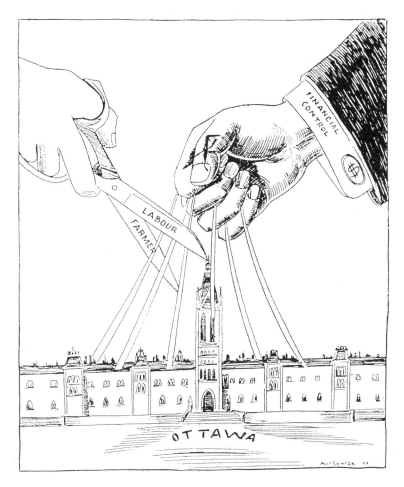

**FREE THE COUNTRY AND INDUSTRY
FROM THE HAND OF THE INVISIBLE GOVERNMENT**

If we do not have public control over finances, we are going to have control of the public by financiers. We can take our choice. *Hansard*, March 4, 1925

ALL THINGS TO ALL MEN

The chameleon (species – Mackenziebus Kingbus): A most interesting and accommodating little creature. If your favourite colour is not visible it will be instantly produced upon the slightest provocation.

Left. The cartoonist supports the speaker's call for public control of finance, and urges farmers and labourers to unite to cut the bonds which tie the government to business interests. The Weekly News, Winnipeg, 16 Oct 1925 Right. The Liberals' minority status meant that Prime Minister King needed the support of the Progressive party in the West. At the same time he could not alienate his supporters in Central Canada or the Maritimes. Compromise, ambiguity and flexibility were among the qualities he needed for survival. National Archives of Canada C-29624

THE TEMPTER

Ever since 1921 King had been trying to win the support of the Progressive party. The Western cartoonist warns voters to be wary of his election promises. The Grain Growers' Guide, *Winnipeg, 21 Oct 1925*

MASTERPIECES
THE RIVALS: It's going to be a true likeness.

HOW WOULD UNCLE SAM VOTE?

Left. Party leaders like to paint the worst possible pictures of their opponents. The Evening Telegram, *Toronto, 18 Sep 1925* **Right.** *Uncle Sam appears to favour King's low tariff policy. In the 1925 election 46 percent of Canadians supported Meighen's strong protectionist platform, but his weakness in the Prairies and in Quebec cost him the election. King governed with support from the Progressives.* The Evening Telegram, *Toronto, 2 Oct 1925*

M. Meighen sue sang et eau pour apprendre le français dans le but de gagner le coeur de la province de Québec comme il a gagné celui d'Armanda.

LE TRAFIQUANT DE CHAIR HUMAINE
En voulez-vous du Meighen impérialiste? Votez pour les candidates de M. Patenaude.

Left. Mr. Meighen sweats blood and water to learn French in order to win the heart of the province of Quebec as he won that of Armanda. [tr.] Meighen's support for conscription in 1917 made it difficult for him to win support in Quebec. Armand Lavergne was an extreme opponent of conscription during the First World War and no friend of Meighen. Le Cri de Québec, 31 July 1925 Right. THE DEALER IN HUMAN FLESH. Do you want anything to do with imperialist Meighen? Vote for the candidates of Mr. Patenaude. [tr.] The cartoonist reminds voters that Conservative leader Meighen, who had supported conscription during the First World War, was still an ardent imperialist ready to send Canadians overseas. Le Soleil, Quebec, 23 Oct 1925

Precedents, poetry, praise, ridicule, oratory and logic
were used plentifully in the wooing of the Progressives.

SPORT

*Left. After the 1925 election King's only hope of avoiding defeat in Parliament was to win the support of the Progressives, who held the balance of power. In the Throne Speech he promised such things as a farm loan program, old age pensions and the completion of the Hudson Bay Railway. The Grain Growers' Guide, Winnipeg, 3 Feb 1926 **Right.** Regulation of the sport of boxing became more important as bouts were increasingly arranged by promoters and governed by economics, rather than athleticism. The Montreal Daily Star, 23 Sep 1926*

PROTECT THE CHILDREN
Why not make a clean sweep while at it?

Left. *A Conservative newspaper makes a clear call for censorship. Many of the newspapers and magazines in question came from the United States.* The Montreal Daily Star, *4 Mar 1926* **Right.** *Some working-class families were unable to survive unless children contributed to the family income. In 1931 less than half of the nation's young people went to school beyond the ninth grade. Some employers preferred child labour because young workers were paid less and could be more easily controlled.* One Big Union Bulletin, *Winnipeg, 12 Aug 1926*

THE SURPRISE PARTY

The illegal export of liquor to the United States helped Canada achieve a favourable balance of trade. The bad news was that the "rumrunners" filled their trucks and boats with a return cargo of smuggled goods. Evidence of corruption in the Montreal customs district forced Prime Minister King to resign. The Grain Growers' Guide, *Winnipeg, 1 June 1926*

"YES, I SUPPORT BOTH PARTIES"

BOOTLEGGER: That's the slogan! The dryer you keep 'em, the more I can sell 'em.

Left. During the investigation of a customs scandal a major distillery stated that it gave money to both major parties. The cartoonist suggests that neither of the major parties can be trusted. Montreal Witness and Canadian Homestead, *1 Sep 1926* **Right.** *Quebec and British Columbia abandoned prohibition in 1920. The other provinces followed suit, but at the time this cartoon was produced Ontario was still dry. Ontario election pamphlet, 1926*

STRIPPING OUR VIRGIN FORESTS

THE SMOKE SCREEN

Left. *Opposition in Nova Scotia to the export of raw logs increased in the 1920s.* The Halifax Herald, *12 Mar 1926* **Right.** *When King resigned because of the customs scandal he asked Governor-General Byng to dissolve Parliament so that he could call an election. Instead Byng asked Meighen to form a government. Meighen did so but was defeated in Parliament. In the ensuing election King claimed that Byng's actions were unconstitutional. This cartoon suggests that the "King-Byng-Thing" was a smokescreen King created to cover his role in the customs scandal.* The Halifax Herald, *11 July 1926*

LA JEUNE PREMIÈRE DU CIRQUE BLEU

MLLE PROTECTION: J'ai pourtant eu des succès dans mon jeune temps. Pourquoi qu'on me rit au nez aujourd'hui? **L'IMPRESARIO TITUR**, songeur: Elle est tout de même un peu fripée notre jeune première..

WAITING FOR THE VERDICT

Left. THE YOUNG STAR OF THE CONSERVATIVE CIRCUS. MISS PROTECTION: I did have some success in my youth. Why do they laugh in my face now? IMPRESARIO TITUR [Arthur Meighen], pensive: Our young star is a little the worse for wear. [tr.] In three previous elections Meighen used his support for a protective tariff as the main plank in his campaign. In the 1926 election he focused on the customs scandal but lost once more. Le Canada, Montreal, 13 Sep 1926 **Right.** *This Ontario cartoon contrasts Meighen's loyalty to Britain with King's strong American connections.* The Evening Telegram, *Toronto, 14 Sep 1926*

EQUAL PARTNERS ALL

The Imperial Conference held in London in 1926 resulted in the Balfour Report, which recognized the Dominions as "autonomous communities within the British Empire equal in status ... though united in a common allegiance to the Crown, and freely associated as members of the British Commonwealth of Nations." The Grain Growers' Guide, Winnipeg, *Winnipeg, 15 Dec 1926*

BADLY IN NEED OF PRUNING

In 1926 the Senate vetoed King's bill to establish old age pensions. King wanted to make the Senate more responsive to the will of the people and threatened Senate reform. In 1927 the Senate passed the Old Age Pension Bill, and King dropped his controversial plans for reform. The Grain Growers' Guide, Winnipeg, *15 Nov 1927*

THE SOLID KEYSTONE
It is more solid and useful than ever and is
not in need of substitution or tinkering.

"GOING IN"
UNCLE SAM: "John's making a mistake in not going in now with us, Jack."

Left. A Dominion–provincial conference was held in November 1927. Justice Minister Ernest Lapointe proposed a Canadian amending procedure for the Constitution but his proposal was defeated. Britain would retain the power to amend Canada's Constitution for another 65 years. The Montreal Daily Star, 25 Oct 1927 ***Right.*** *British investment in Canada remained at the same level throughout the interwar years while American investment steadily increased. Mineral production in Canada doubled in the 1920s and the production of pulp and paper and hydroelectric power more than tripled.* The Toronto Daily Star, 19 Feb 1927

LA FEMME MODERNE CHEZ LE PHOTOGRAPHE

LE PHOTOGRAPHE: Madame veut-elle que je la pose comme un homme. Veut-elle sourire comme une femme? Veut-elle avoir l'air respectable ou mondain?
MADAME: Posez-moi telle que je suis. En femme moderne qui a les manières masculines. Mon mari m'aime comme ça. **LE PHOTOGRAPHE**: Il n'est pas difficile. Allons! ne bougez plus. Ça y est, madame... est la mode.

THE MODERN WOMAN AT THE PHOTOGRAPHER'S. THE PHOTOGRAPHER: Would madam like me to pose her like a man? Would she like to smile like a woman? Would she like to have a respectable or a worldly air? WOMAN: Pose me as I am, as a modern woman who has masculine ways. My husband likes me like that. PHOTOGRAPHER: That's not difficult. Now, don't move. That's it, madam, that's the style. [tr.] The word "flapper" was used to describe young women who were bold and unconventional in their actions and dress. Le Canard, Montreal, 16 Jan 1927

THE CHANGED MARRIAGE SERVICE
MODERN BRIDE: "Gee! We dropped *that* word long ago."

KING THE THIMBLERIG
Knock him down and he bobs right up

Left. The Anglican Church revised the Church of England prayer book to exclude the word "obey" from the bride's marriage vows. The Montreal Daily Star, 9 Feb 1927 **Right.** Mackenzie King was Canada's longest-serving prime minister, mainly because of his cautious approach to controversial issues such as free trade and conscription. By not taking a clear stand he made it difficult for his political enemies to attack him. The Grain Growers' Guide, Winnipeg, 1 Dec 1927

A LITTLE CO-OPERATION AND THE GAME IS WON

PARTAGE DE LA POMME?

Left. *Co-operatives were a practical solution to some of the problems of rural Canada. Members of the various pools obtained better prices for their grain and other products by selling it through their co-operatives rather than fighting their own way through the competitive system.* The Scoop Shovel, *Winnipeg, Mar 1927* **Right.** SHARING THE APPLE? *In 1907 Great Britain, Newfoundland and Canada submitted the undefined boundaries of Labrador for consideration by the Judicial Committee of the Privy Council. In 1927 the Committee finally decided in favour of Newfoundland, much to the dismay of Quebec and the apparent relief of Madam Privy Council ("now leave me in peace").* La Presse, *Montreal, 5 Mar 1927*

THE "NETT" RESULTS

THE SLOW PICTURE SHOW

For a number of years the federal government issued an unlimited number of cannery and fishing licences. Salmon runs declined and fishing was eventually limited in order to let enough salmon reach the spawning grounds. The cartoonists disapprove of a politically managed fishing industry. The Vancouver Herald, *27 Sep and 20 Nov 1927*

THE KEY TO THE FUTURE OF CANADA
Keep a tight grip on it.

Canada's future lay in her immense store of natural resources. While the Americans pushed for the development of hydroelectric power on the St. Lawrence River, the King government opposed the export of Canadian power to the United States. The Montreal Daily Star, *16 Jan 1928*

A TRAGIC SITUATION

AT THE KNOTHOLE

Left. Tuberculosis, the "white plague," killed 8,000 people a year in Canada. Poor nutrition and poor housing and working conditions encouraged the spread of the disease. The working poor, who were the main victims, rarely had access to adequate treatment. The Halifax Herald, 9 May 1928 **Right.** At the 1928 Olympic games in Amsterdam Vancouver sprinter Percy Williams became "the fastest human being" when he won gold medals in the 100- and 200-metre sprints. This achievement sparked intense national pride and Canadian–American sports rivalry. Williams' coach, Bob Granger, had to pay his own way to the Olympics. The Granger fund was set up to help pay his expenses. The Vancouver Daily Province, 2 Aug 1928

MAKING HIS TITLE CLEAR
T. L. CHURCH, MP: I'm adding these words of truth just
to explain your general attitude, Mr. Lapointe.

STILL ADRIFT

Left. A resident of Quebec, Ontario or Prince Edward Island could obtain a divorce only by means of a private bill passed by Parliament. The procedure favoured the wealthy, and Canada had the lowest divorce rate in the western world. While Roman Catholic Quebec opposed divorce on principle, Ontario would gain a divorce court in 1930. The Evening Telegram, *Toronto, 1 May 1928* **Right.** *In 1927 the federal government introduced pensions for people over the age of 70 who passed a means test. As the provinces had to match the federal funding, poorer provinces were unable to participate. Some elderly people in the Maritimes eventually received reduced pensions in the 1930s.* The Halifax Herald, *16 Jun 1928*

EQUALITY OF STATUS WITHIN EQUALITY OF STATUS

RETOUR EN VITESSE

Left. In 1928 the Six Nations of Brantford, Ontario, renounced allegiance to Canada and to the British Crown in a declaration of independence. The hereditary chiefs of the Six Nations compare their desire for independence within Canada to Canada's desire for independence within the Commonwealth. The Montreal Daily Star, *5 July 1928* **Right.** *A SPEEDY RETURN. The Ku Klux Klan was a white supremacist secret society which originated in the southern United States. It operated in some Canadian provinces in the 1920s and 1930s, targeting blacks, Jews, foreigners and Catholics. In 1928 the federal government deported one American Klan organizer to the United States.* La Presse, Montreal, 21 July 1928

DÉCISION

THE JAILS CAN'T HOLD HIM

Left. The British North America Act contained a section dealing with qualifications for membership in the Senate. In 1927 five Alberta women asked the Supreme Court of Canada if the term "qualified persons" included women. The court decided that women were not eligible. The "Alberta five" decided to appeal the decision to the Privy Council in England. La Presse, *Montreal, 28 Apr 1928* **Right.** *Federal laws against smuggling alcohol to the United States apparently were not popular in Nova Scotia. Juries tended to acquit people caught smuggling.* The Halifax Herald, *3 Mar 1928*

MILLIONS FOR WAR MATERIALS — NOT A CENT FOR THE LIVING VICTIMS OF THE GREAT (CAPITALIST) WAR

Communists blamed capitalism for the First World War. A cartoonist for a communist newspaper contrasts the willingness of profiteers to build monuments to the dead with their reluctance to support government pensions for impoverished and wounded survivors. The Young Worker, *Toronto, Feb 1928*

NOMENCLATURE
Stations on the Hudson Bay Railway are now being named.
These appropriate names are suggested to aid the authorities.

WHEN THE HUDSON BAY PORT IS OPENED

Left. *Western farmers called for the development of a railway to Hudson Bay, which would provide an alternate route for exporting grain. This Eastern Canadian cartoon makes fun of their proposal.* The Montreal Daily Star, *11 April 1928*
Right. *In 1928 the federal government built a railway to Fort Churchill on Hudson Bay. Westerners were highly optimistic that the Hudson Bay Railway would become a major corridor for Western exports and imports.* The Montreal Daily Star, *31 Oct 1928*

THE CRUX OF THE GREAT WATERWAYS SITUATION

Bypassing rapids and waterfalls along the St. Lawrence River would allow ocean-going vessels to reach the heart of the continent. American cities along the Great Lakes and farmers in the American mid-west were interested in the proposed seaway because it would provide cheaper transportation for their products. The Grain Growers' Guide, *Montreal, 1 May 1928*

THE EMPTY PACKING CASES
Just as big as daddy.

THAT ACQUISITIVE INSTINCT

Left. King promoted the idea of national independence but he did not accept all of the responsibilities of nationhood. He feared that a strong military would draw Canada into the defence of the Empire, and made drastic cuts to the military budget after the war. The Montreal Daily Star, *31 May 1928* **Right.** *More and more women were entering the workforce in non-traditional roles.* The Vancouver Sun, *5 Dec 1928.*

THE COUNTRY THAT ISN'T SO

In 1927 Canada established embassies in Washington, Paris and Tokyo. Some Canadians, who placed the Empire first, wanted Britain to continue looking after Canada's foreign affairs. The Canadian Magazine, *Toronto, Mar 1929*

ANOTHER BUILDING STONE FOR CANADA

JUSTICE, AND A DETERRENT

Left. This cartoonist saw American plans to raise tariffs in a positive light. The hardships created by the tariffs gave Canada a fresh incentive to become a nation and look after her own affairs. The Vancouver Sun, 4 Jul 1929 Right. Canadians liked to compare their "peace, order and good government" with the higher crime rate in the United States and the slower pace of the American legal system. The Vancouver Sun, 26 Jun 1929

QU'IMPORTE QUE FEMMES ET ENFANTS AIENT FAIM!

L'OUVRIER BLESSÉ: Attendre encore quinze semaines! Mais ma famille n'a rien à manger, je n'ai ni crédit ni revenus! **LE PORTIER**: Qu'est-ce que vous voulez que ça me fasse. J'ai mon salaire, moi, et c'est tout ce qui m'intéresse. D'ailleurs la loi de M. Taschereau ne peut rien faire de plus.

WHAT DOES IT MATTER IF WOMEN AND CHILDREN ARE HUNGRY! THE INJURED WORKER: Wait another fifteen weeks! But my family has nothing to eat. I have no credit and no income. THE DOORMAN: What do you want me to do? I have my salary and that's all that interests me. Moreover, Mr. Taschereau's law can do no more. [tr.] Even during the period of business prosperity from 1924 to 1929, the average Canadian did little more than meet expenses from day to day. Few were able to save for periods of illness or injury and there was no workers' compensation or unemployment insurance. Le Goglu, Montreal, 20 Nov 1929

ROMANCE SANS PAROLES

Left. In 1927 the Mine Workers' Union joined a group of independent Canadian unions in Montreal to form the All-Canadian Congress of Labour (ACCL). This nationalistic left-wing group blamed American-controlled unions for many of the problems facing the Canadian labour force. The Confédération de travailleurs catholiques du Canada (CTCC), a more conservative Quebec organization with similar concerns, had been formed in 1921. The Canadian Unionist, Nov 1929
Right. STORY WITHOUT WORDS. Inexpensive electrical power was very attractive to industry, and the United States was prepared to take what it wanted from Canada. This cartoon opposes the sale of Quebec electric power to the United States. Le Goglu, Montreal, 13 Dec 1929

HE JUST QUIETLY PLOUGHS ON

THE WAY THE WIND'S BLOWING

Left. The cartoonist suggests that Canada should reject both American and British ways in favour of a uniquely Canadian approach. The Vancouver Sun, *16 Dec 1929* **Right.** The United States was in the process of raising high tariffs against Canadian agricultural and farm products. Prime Minister King planned to retaliate by diverting trade to Britain and lowering duties on goods coming from Britain, while Conservative opposition leader Bennett wanted to introduce tariffs against American goods. Uncle Sam would lose either way. The Vancouver Daily Province, *26 Jun 1929*

WELL, IT SHOULDN'T BE LONG NOW

A LESSON NEVER LEARNED

Left. The Kitsilano reserve in British Columbia was located on a valuable piece of land near downtown Vancouver. Vancouver wanted part of the land for a bridge and park. The Vancouver Sun, 26 Mar 1929 **Right.** A downturn in the stock market began in September 1929 and climaxed on October 29. Three days before "Black Tuesday" the Conservative cartoonist cautions speculators drawn like moths to the flame of financial gain. The Montreal Daily Star, 26 Oct 1929

THE SUPPLY LINE

Prohibition in the United States created a "rumrunning" industry in Canada. Canadians were more than willing to export liquor, even though its importation into the United States was illegal. The Grain Growers' Guide, *Winnipeg, 23 Nov 1927*

THE HOLIDAY SEASON
Miss Agnes MacPhail indulges in day reveries and midsummer night dreams.

THE HOLIDAY SEASON
What can be more delightful than a day or two off speeding in the fresh country air amidst the restful quiet and beautiful scenery?

Left. In 1921 Agnes MacPhail was the first woman elected to Parliament. She supported many causes, including disarmament. The Montreal Daily Star, *6 Aug 1929* **Right.** *The proliferation of billboards eventually led most governments to restrict their use.* The Montreal Daily Star, *27 July 1929*

EST-CE QUE LA FEMME VEUT REMPLACER L'HOMME???...

MADAME: Bonjour. Ma conférence sur les Droits de la Femme a eu du succès, mon Comité a fait placer 25 jeunes filles dans des bureaux d'avocats, 38 sont nommées caissières dans les banques. 75 ont obtenu des positions dans de grands magasins et bientôt nous aurons des "policewomen" et des conductrices de tramways. Si on peut avoir le droit de vote et se faire élire "échevine", "avocate", "députée"... faire valoir nos qualités supérieures, la femme... **MONSIEUR**: ... la femme... ne sera plus une mère de famille, elle aura trop d'occupations. Tu as ton club, tu fumes, tu... tu... Tiens! viens donc souper... mon chéri de femme, ta p'tite chatte de mari a tout préparé.

DO WOMEN WANT TO REPLACE MEN? WIFE: My conference on women's rights was a success. My committee has placed 25 young women in lawyer's offices, 38 as cashiers in the bank, 75 in department stores, and soon we will have policewomen and female tram conductors. If we can have the right to vote and to become alderwomen, lawyers, deputies... to have our superior qualities valued, women... HUSBAND: ... the woman... will no longer be the mother of the family; she will have too many jobs. You have your club, you smoke... you... Come have your dinner, my dear wife. Your little pet husband has prepared everything. [tr.] This Quebec cartoon makes fun of a female activist and her long-suffering husband. Le Canard, Montreal, 6 Jan 1929

ANOTHER GOAL REACHED

"It is the women themselves that have gained this victory for their sex."

NO MORE PRIVACY

And now a machine that enables one to see in the dark.

Left. In July 1929 the Person's Case was argued before the Privy Council in England. The court reversed the Canadian Supreme Court decision of 1928 and ruled that women were eligible for appointment as senators. The Montreal Daily Star, *19 Feb 1930* **Right.** *A cartoonist for one of Montreal's largest newspapers saw modern inventions and practices as a major invasion of privacy.* The Montreal Daily Star, *10 Feb 1930*

OVER-PRODUCTION

The Depression of the 1930s really started in the Prairies in 1928, when a world glut of wheat led to a serious drop in prices. The stock market crash of October 1929 made the situation even worse. This Western Canadian cartoon blames the Depression on the profit system. The Scoop-Shovel, Winnipeg, Apr 1930

WHAT CAN WOMEN DO TO COMBAT THE HIGH COST OF SICKNESS?

Women felt that men ignored many of society's problems. Now that they had the vote they were urged to organize and vote as a group to improve such things as the health care system. The Chatelaine, *Toronto, Jan 1930*

THE RED MENACE

POLITICAL HUMAN NATURE

Left. *The Maritime economy was weak, and it became weaker with the onset of the Depression. There was widespread unemployment and wages were low. Mine workers in Nova Scotia who tried to organize a union were branded as part of a foreign conspiracy and met with little success.* The Halifax Herald, *11 Apr 1930*
Right. *As a federal election approached, the Conservative opposition argued that the federal government should give money to the provincial governments to pay for unemployment relief. Five of the provincial governments were Conservative. Under intense heckling King lost his temper and stated that he would not give the Tory governments a five-cent piece. His comment was to cost him dearly in the 1930 election.* Manitoba Free Press, Winnipeg, *8 Apr 1930*

QU'EST-CE QUE ÇA PEUT BIEN LUI FAIRE?

Quand Québec a lutté pour garder le Labrador, mal défendu et que nous avons perdu, M. King n'a rien dit ni rien fait pour nous protéger. Il a ruiné notre agriculture, nos industries, passé l'infâme loi du divorce. Qu'est-ce que ça pouvait lui faire que nous perdions encore les immenses richesses minières et hydro-électriques du Labrador? Mettons un homme de coeur à sa place.

UP IT GOES

Why not: "A Protection and Canada First" policy for Canada? "Washington has found protection so successful and profitable that the tariff wall has been made still higher, making the inequalities in trade against Canada still greater."

Left. WHAT WILL THAT MEAN TO HIM? When Quebec struggled to keep Labrador, which was badly defended and which we lost, Mr. King said nothing and did nothing to protect us. He has ruined our agriculture and our industries, and passed the infamous divorce law. What could it mean to him that we lost the immense mineral and hydroelectric riches of Labrador? Let's put a man with a heart in his place. [tr.] A Quebec nationalist newspaper reminds its readers that King was in power when Quebec lost Labrador in a border dispute with Newfoundland. Le Goglu, *Montreal, 4 July 1930* **Right.** *As the effects of the Depression deepened, the United States reacted by increasing protective tariffs.* The Montreal Daily Star, *20 June 1930*

THE BENNETT CAFETERIA.

Left. Immigration increased substantially from 1924 to 1929. By September 1929 the economy was moving into a depression. King's failure to quickly stem the flow of immigrants was one of the reasons for his defeat in the 1930 election. The new Bennett government acted quickly to do so, and the policy lasted throughout the depression-ridden 1930s. One Big Union Bulletin, *Winnipeg, 3 Apr 1930* **Right.** *Conservative leader R. B. Bennett promised voters that he would counter recent American tariff increases with high Canadian tariffs. He also promised the unemployed jobs, not relief. The voters bought his over-optimistic promises ("cheese and apple sauce") and gave the Conservatives a majority government.* Winnipeg Free Press, *22 July 1930*

UP AGAINST THE REAL THING

UNCLE SAM: "Well, there's a guy what ain't just a bluffer, anyhow."

BENNETT'S TWENTY MILLIONS

Unemployment is steadily increasing in Canada. The Young Workers can expect nothing for the $20,000,000 that is to be expended as a means of "solving" the unemployment problem. Some lousy soup and the mission house will be the lot of the unemployed young worker unless we organize and fight for work or full maintenance.

Left. Bennett lost little time in raising tariffs on manufactured goods and agricultural products. In the short term he hoped to provide jobs producing the goods formerly imported from the United States; in the long term he hoped that higher tariffs would force the Americans to negotiate new terms with Canada. The Halifax Herald, *27 Sep 1930* **Right.** *The unemployed had previously been considered a municipal responsibility. Now, for the first time, the federal government accepted responsibility for supporting them. This cartoon from a communist newspaper contrasts the amount allotted to the unemployed with that ultimately going to businesses.* The Young Worker, *Toronto, 6 Oct 1930*

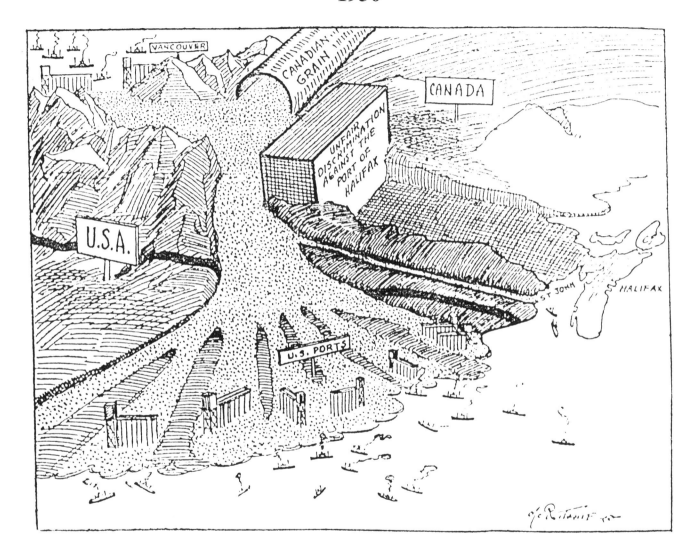

THE GREAT DIVIDE

The Maritime Rights movement of the late 1920s led to improvement of the harbours at Halifax and Saint John, but most Canadian grain exports continued to flow through United States ports. The Halifax Herald, *27 Nov 1930*

BACKSTAGE AT OTTAWA
Its honeymoon of office over, Mr. Bennett and his Ministry find themselves beset by tribulations.

Soon after his election Bennett left for an Imperial Conference in London, where he helped to complete the Statute of Westminster and tried unsuccessfully to negotiate an intra-Imperial trade agreement. On his return he had to confront the major problems facing Canada. Maclean's Magazine, *Toronto, 15 Feb 1931*

FIGHTING A LOSING BATTLE

Left. The impact of hydroelectric projects on the environment is not a new concern in Canada. The Halifax Herald, *5 Mar 1931* **Right.** *Many men who had served their country during the First World War found that they were not needed during the Depression.* The Country Guide, *Feb 1931*

Left-wing groups contrasted the full industrialization and employment in the government-run economy of the Soviet Union with the reduced industrial production and increased unemployment in capitalist countries. Few Canadians opted for the communist system, but the Depression shook their faith in the Liberal and Conservative parties and new parties emerged. Canadian Labor Defender, *Toronto, May 1931*

NO FOOLING
Hard times demand stern measures.

WOULD PUT ENEMIES OF HEALTH TO FLIGHT

Left. Some union leaders were communist and most were labelled as such whether they were or not, particularly when they opposed cuts or acted to protect workers' interests. In August 1931 the government arrested nine party leaders in Toronto and charged them with seditious conspiracy. Eight of the accused were found guilty. The Halifax Herald, *13 Aug 1931* **Right.** *The radio had a great impact on shut-ins and people living in isolated areas.* The Halifax Herald, *9 Apr 1931*

BENNETT'S "PEACE, ORDER AND GOOD GOVERNMENT"

LES INJUSTICES DE M. BENNETT
C'est toujours l'ouvrier qui paye.

Left. In 1931 coal miners from Estevan, Saskatchewan, went on strike to win recognition for their union. The mine owners sought the help of politicians and the RCMP to break the union. The police drew their revolvers and opened fire on a strikers' parade, killing three miners. Bennett called on Canadians to suppress with an "iron heel" any sympathy for the union. Canadian Labor Defender, *Toronto, Nov 1931* **Right.** *MR. BENNETT'S INJUSTICES. It's always the worker who pays. [tr.] High tariffs meant that Canadians had to pay more for imported goods. Bennett hoped that the protective tariffs would persuade Canadian manufacturers to increase production and invest their profits in job creation. This Liberal cartoon suggests that Bennett's policies favoured the rich at the expense of the workers.* L'Action Libérale, *Montreal, 4 July 1931*

HE WONDERS WHY THE GOODS DON'T MOVE
Canadian exports were nearly $23,000,000 less in Feb. 1931 than in the same month in 1930.

Canada was hit hard by the Depression. Most of the products of Canada's farms, forests and mines were produced for export, and the high tariffs erected by Bennett only added to the declining world interest in Canada's staples. Winnipeg Free Press, *15 Apr 1931*

THE RAID ON BEAUHARNOIS
The commencement of operations on the construction of the Beauharnois Canal.

In 1931 evidence emerged that the Liberal party had received a $700,000 donation from the Beauharnois Power Corporation in return for a federal hydroelectric development licence. King maintained that he knew nothing about campaign funds and had not been influenced by the donation. The Country Guide, Winnipeg, *Sep 1931*

CELLE QUI TRAVAILLE   CELLE QUI NE TRAVAILLE PAS

THE ONE WHO WORKS AND THE ONE WHO DOESN'T WORK. In 1931 fewer than 17 per cent of women worked outside the home. The cartoonist suggests that housewives work even harder than those who are employed. La Presse, Montreal, 31 Jan 1931

"CANADIANS?" HE'LL SHOW THEM

REACHING THE GOAL

Left. In the 1931 census Canadians were once again forced to declare their ethnic origins, a process that went counter to the growing spirit of Canadian nationalism. Winnipeg Free Press, 12 May 1931 **Right.** *The Statute of Westminster formalized Canada's transition from colony to autonomous nation and gave Canadians control over their foreign policy. Winnipeg Free Press, 15 May 1931*

BAPTISTE N'EN VEUT PAS

BAPTISTE: Non, merci, la mère; ça serait mortel pour ma langue, c'fricot-là!

Left. BAPTISTE DOESN'T WANT ANYTHING TO DO WITH IT. BAPTISTE: No thanks, mother, that stew would be fatal for my language. [tr.] Private radio stations were flooding the country with American programs. Quebeckers feared that a proposed government-owned broadcasting system would destroy the French language. The solution was a publicly owned network (the Canadian Radio Broadcasting Corporation) which broadcast in French and in English. La Presse, Montreal, 27 Apr 1932 **Right.** *Opposition to a publicly owned broadcasting system came from privately owned radio stations and from conservative groups who opposed government ownership.* The Evening Telegram, *Toronto, 17 May 1932*

ANOTHER MOUTH TO FEED

YET MR. BENNETT WHISTLES

**'TWAS THE LOAD THAT FATHER CARRIED
THAT MADE HIM BEND SO LOW**

Left. In the 1930 election Bennett made a lot of promises. The cartoonist shows him "whistling past the graveyard" of the promises he was unable to keep. The Halifax Chronicle, *10 Dec 1932* **Right.** *Many people who had jobs wanted the government to reduce taxes and spend less money.* The Evening Telegram, *Toronto, 11 Apr 1932*

ALL TOGETHER BOYS

R. B. Bennett raised tariffs starting in 1930, but his long-term plan was to strike a deal with Britain and the other Commonwealth nations for an Imperial preference system. The Commonwealth nations would have a common high tariff for non-members and a lower tariff for members. Bennett hoped that such a plan would help revitalize the economy and end the Depression. Minor moves in this direction were made at an Imperial Economic Conference held in Ottawa in July. The Vernon News, *21 July 1932*

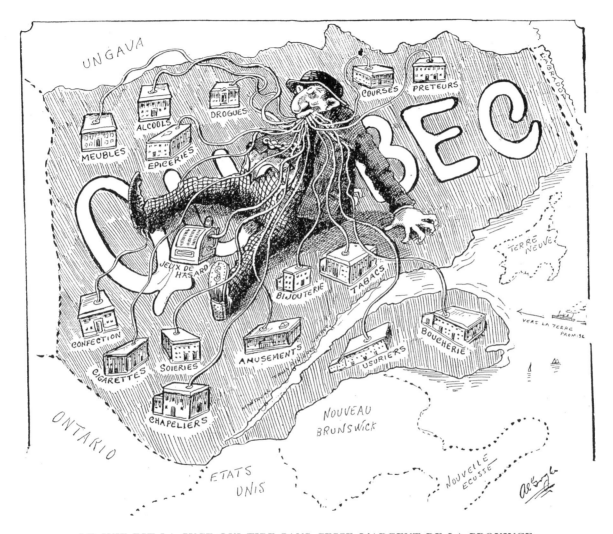

LE JUIF EST LA SUCE QUI TIRE SANS CESSE L'ARGENT DE LA PROVINCE

THE JEW UNCEASINGLY SUCKS MONEY FROM THE PROVINCE. A commentary which accompanied this cartoon claimed that the "Jewish octopus" had seized all the economic power in Quebec and was bleeding the province of its riches. Such anti-Semitic propaganda helps to explain the indifference of many Canadians to the flood of Jews seeking to escape Nazi persecution in Germany. Between 1933 and 1939 Canada would accept only 4,000 Jewish refugees. Le Goglu, Montreal, 8 Jan 1932

ALL TAKE AND NO GIVE

Canada exported 80 per cent of the production of her mines, farms and forests. When US president Hoover increased tariffs to protect American producers during the Depression he set off a tariff war throughout the world, and the demand for Canadian staples declined. Prime Minister Bennett joined the rest of the world with a sharp increase in Canada's tariffs. The Vancouver Daily Province, *7 Nov 1932*

ALL ON THE STREETS ON MONDAY

Upper Left. Young people were among the hardest hit by the Depression. Many graduated from school and quickly joined the ranks of the unemployed. Those who left home depended on relief or handouts from soup kitchens. The Young Worker, *Toronto, 30 Aug 1932* **Lower left.** *Some of the unemployed received direct relief. Single homeless men were offered work in camps generally organized by the Canadian army and were given food, shelter and twenty cents per day. Most did not go voluntarily, and those who left were denied all further relief.* The Young Worker, *Toronto, 11 Nov 1932* **Right.** *Many of the unemployed fought against work camps and for work and wages.* Unemployed Worker, *Vancouver, 20 Feb 1932*

TOO COSTLY TO KEEP

Left. *Left wing parties and newspapers helped the unemployed fight for government work projects and relief, and opposed the groups demanding lower taxes. Municipal governments, faced with an inadequate taxation base, made relief as small and demeaning as possible.* The Worker, *Toronto, 3 July 1933* **Right.** *As business declined and unemployment increased, tax revenues decreased. Tremendous pressure was placed on all levels of government to reduce both costs and taxes.* The Halifax Chronicle, *22 Apr 1933*

TIME FOR SANE TREATMENT

Unless the doctors throw away their quack remedies and slow poisons, open the window and let in some fresh air, the poor patient hasn't a chance of recovery.

THE UNLOVED CHILD

Left. World trade declined as nations sought to protect their domestic markets from foreign competition by increasing protective tariffs. To remedy the situation nations would have to cooperate in reducing tariffs that were strangling trade. The Halifax Chronicle, 11 Oct 1933 Right. The price of wheat dropped dramatically during the Depression as the world's major wheat-producing nations competed in selling their surplus grain. The Halifax Chronicle, 20 Sep 1933

A MARITIMER SPEAKS HIS MIND   **IN SEARCH OF CANADIANS**

Left. Since the start of the Depression in 1929, timber, steel, fish, coal and agricultural production in the Maritimes had fallen anywhere from 38 to 75 per cent. The West did not do much better. High tariffs helped protect the industries of Central Canada, but even there production fell by one third. Maclean's Magazine, *Toronto, 1 Feb 1933* **Right.** *Instead of taking pride in their own achievements Canadians too often made heroes of their English and American counterparts.* The Canadian Magazine, *Toronto, June 1933*

THE STRONG LONG ARM REACHES AND CLUTCHES
A warning, or, another "pestilential vulture" disappears.

MORE KIDNAP TROUBLE

Left. Severe prison sentences and lashing were considered the best way to control the drug trade in the 1930s. The Montreal Daily Star, *23 Oct 1933*
***Right.** As the policies of the traditional parties failed to end the Depression, people started to consider new parties. The Co-operative Commonwealth Federation advocated a broad range of social services to look after the sick, injured, aged and unemployed. Bennett and other politicians took and implemented some of the ideas of the CCF.* The Vancouver Daily Province, *11 Aug 1933*

THE HOARY TROJAN HORSE TRICK AGAIN
JOHNNY CANUCK: Tut, tut, Woodsworth! I'm surprised that you should attempt to put over such an old trick on me!

Marxist doctrine and the Canadian Communist Party held little appeal for most Canadians. The newly formed Co-operative Commonwealth Federation was far more successful. Although led by socialists, members believed in parliamentary democracy and sought to reform, not destroy, capitalism. This Conservative cartoon argues that CCF leader Woodsworth plans to use his party as a Trojan horse to introduce communist principles. The Montreal Daily Star, *21 Sep 1933*

SUPPOSING THE GIRLS BECAME ARTICULATE TOO!

REHABILITATION, OR, FROM DESPAIR TO HOPE
"The wolf refused to leave his door, so he packed and left the wolf."

Left. During the Depression most employers stopped hiring women. Men were seen as the breadwinners, and women were supposed to marry and be taken care of by their husbands. With marriage rates dropping, many women were forced to live with their parents, work at poorly paid work, or worse. The Vancouver Sun, *10 Jan 1934* **Right.** *Drought was a serious problem in the southern Prairies in the 1930s. The government provided assistance to farmers willing to relocate to less arid areas farther north.* The Montreal Daily Star, *17 Sep 1934*

PLAIN ENGLISH
PREMIER R. B. BENNETT: "No, Mr. Armand Lavergne, Canada's money's only going to talk in one language and that's the kind I'm using."

SHOULD THEY DO IT?
ALL THREE—Let's discuss this question of amalgamation on a businesslike basis.

Left. In 1934 Bennett decided to create a privately controlled central bank, the Bank of Canada. Conservative and Liberal members of Parliament from Quebec demanded bilingual currency. Bennett insisted that bills would be printed separately in English and in French. The Evening Telegram, *Toronto, 28 June 1934*
Right. This cartoon suggests that the Prairie provinces could save themselves a lot of money by uniting to form one province. The same was proposed for the Maritime provinces. The idea was not popular among politicians as many of them would be out of a job. The Monetary Times, *Montreal, 14 Apr 1934*

THE STEVENS COMMITTEE IS FURNISHING MOST OF THE NEWS FROM OTTAWA

In 1934 Harry Stevens, minister of trade and commerce in Bennett's government, made a speech attacking large businesses for unfair practices. Some businesses cut wages and operated sweatshops in order to survive. The Country Guide, *Winnipeg, Apr 1934*

A STUDY IN CONTRASTS

LATE SPRING CLEANING

Left. Canadians and Americans liked to contrast their 3,000 miles of undefended border and their peaceful resolution of disputes with the heavily defended European borders and the inability of Europeans to settle their disputes peacefully. The Hamilton Spectator, 4 Aug 1934 **Right.** *Concern over sex and violence in films is nothing new. The Hamilton Spectator, 28 July 1934*

HIGHWAY HAZARDS

DÉFENDEZ VOTRE JOURNAL!
Groupez-vous autour du journal qui défend
les intérêts des travailleurs!

Left. *The end of prohibition in North America brought an increase in deaths and injuries caused by alcohol-related road accidents.* The Monetary Times, *Montreal, 4 Aug 1934* **Right.** DEFEND YOUR NEWSPAPER! *Support the newspaper that defends the interests of the workers! [tr.] Under Section 98 of the Criminal Code the federal government banned "unlawful associations" that advocated the use of force to bring about change. Civil liberty groups objected to the Code's broad definition of sedition and supported those imprisoned under Section 98. When the government released eight Communist leaders in 1934 more than 17,000 people attended a mass rally at Maple Leaf Gardens in Toronto.* La Vie Ouvrière, *Quebec, 10 Nov 1934*

THE SPIRIT OF '35

THE NEW DEAL QUINTUPLETS
Latest picture of the Ottawa quintuplets with their proud parents. This extraordinary family is creating widespread interest and the health of the babies is being closely watched by the populace at large

Left. In early 1935 Bennett announced a "New Deal" for the Canadian people. His reforms were modeled on President Roosevelt's dramatic attempts to fight the Depression in the United States by strong government intervention in the economy. In Canada such reforms were associated with the Co-operative Commonwealth Federation. CCF leader Woodsworth appears highly suspicious of Bennett's and King's sudden conversion to his reform policies. The Halifax Chronicle, *29 Jan 1935* **Right.** *Bennett hoped that his New Deal legislation would increase his chance of re-election. The cartoonist uses the recent birth of the Dionne quintuplets in Ontario to focus attention on five of the reforms associated with the New Deal.* The Montreal Daily Star, *25 Jan 1935*

"KEEP THE HOME FIRES BURNING"

The rearmament programs of many world governments had a positive effect on Canada's mining, smelting and steel industries. The cartoonist suggests that the capitalists of the world will benefit the most from rearmament. The Worker, *Toronto, 28 Mar 1935*

L'OGRE

SAVIEZ-VOUS QUE... Pour assurer la subsistance de ce gargantua moderne l'état doit le nourrir à raison de $2,00 par seconde?

Left. THE OGRE. DID YOU KNOW THAT... *to assure the survival of this modern gargantua the state must feed him at the rate of $2.00 a second? [tr.] In the 1930s the different levels of government spent nearly a billion dollars (a huge sum at the time) on direct relief to the unemployed.* La Patrie Dimanche, *Montreal, 10 Mar 1935* **Right.** *Men sent to relief camps built roads, cleared land and cut railroad ties. Although their basic needs were met, many resented working in depressing, isolated camps, and struggling taxpayers resented paying for them to do so.* The Vancouver Daily Province, *18 May 1935*

FULL STEAM AHEAD!

In 1935 thousands of frustrated relief camp workers left their camps in the interior of British Columbia and headed for Vancouver. When the federal government failed to respond to their complaints they decided to go to Ottawa. The On-to-Ottawa Trek gathered momentum as the workers headed across the country on freight trains. The Worker, *Toronto, 15 June 1935*

ONLY ONE CHOICE
It's the man or the snake.

"GET BACK INTO THAT CAMP. YOU . . .!"

Left. Bennett ordered the police to stop the Communist-led trekkers in Regina. The Evening Telegram, *6 July 1935* **Right.** *The police attacked the trekkers with baseball bat batons. In the ensuing riot many were injured and one policeman was killed. One hundred and twenty protestors ended up in jail. Eventually the trekkers were offered transportation home. The Dominion Day riot cost Bennett dearly in the ensuing election,* The Worker, *Toronto, 2 July 1935*

IL NOUS LAISSE ÉTOUFFER

Les trusts nous pressurent. Chacun de nous est victime de leur emprise. Mais M. Taschereau-les-Trusts s'en lave les mains, en refusant de nous en délivrer. Quand secouerons-nous le joug de cet hypocrite?

HE IS LETTING US CHOKE. The trusts are squeezing us. Each one of us is a victim of their grip, but Mr. Taschereau [the Liberal premier of Quebec] refuses to deliver us from them. When will we shake off the yoke of this hypocrite? [tr.] The cost of basic items such as bread, milk, electricity and coal in Quebec was controlled by a small number of companies, many of which were owned by Americans and English Canadians. Some young Liberals called for the provincial government to nationalize the trusts. La Province, Montreal, 26 Sep 1935

THE OLD MEDICINE MAN AND THE NEW CURE-ALL

MEDICINE MAN: Lade-e-s and Gents.–I have no testimonials from economists or financiers, and no one ever tried it, but I assure you that it's a MAR-R-VELOUS remedy for all your ills. PASSING DUCK: Quack, quack, quack, quack!

HE'S HEAVY ON HER FEET

Left. *Alberta preacher William Aberhart successfully promoted a novel approach to the Depression which he called Social Credit. The idea sounded simple. Food and consumer goods were readily available but people did not have the money to buy them. A Social Credit government would give everyone 25 dollars a month. Aberhart was elected in a landslide but his something-for-nothing ideas were never implemented.* The Montreal Daily Star, *18 June 1935* **Right.** *In a sense King had been lucky to lose the 1930 federal election to Bennett, who had to deal with the Depression. When Bennett's best efforts failed the voters were ready to give King another chance to run the country.* The Halifax Chronicle, *18 Sep 1935*

SMILING THROUGH

"AFTER YOU MY DEAR ALPHONSE—"

Left. *Unlike Bennett, King believed that the best way to end the Depression was to reduce tariffs by negotiating trade agreements with other countries. His 1935 agreement with Roosevelt was Canada's first trade treaty with the Americans since 1854.* The Hamilton Spectator, *16 Nov 1935* **Right.** *In October 1935 Italian dictator Mussolini invaded Ethiopia. Bennett encouraged Canada's delegate to the League of Nations to lead an attempt to apply oil sanctions against Italy. In the October federal election Bennett was defeated. Newly elected Mackenzie King feared that strong international action might divide the country, and withdrew Canada's support for sanctions.* The Vancouver Sun, *4 Dec 1935*

LE CHEVALIER
DUPLESSIS: Qu'on ose y toucher!

THE KNIGHT. DUPLESSIS: Let anyone dare to touch her! [tr.] In 1936 the federal government wanted to amend the Constitution and introduce federal unemployment insurance. The premiers of both Ontario and Quebec opposed the move on the grounds of provincial autonomy and the likelihood that they would have to pay the bulk of the cost. La Patrie Dimanche, Montreal, 13 Feb 1936

A RIGHT TRUE AND VALIANT KNIGHT

THE CAUSE OF IT ALL

Left. *William Aberhart and his Social Credit government in Alberta had been elected in a landslide in 1935. With evangelical zeal Aberhart promised to seize control of the financial system and issue a "national dividend" to every citizen in the province. While most of his economic reforms were disallowed by the federal government, he did provide Alberta with an honest government.* The Albertan, *Calgary, 29 Feb 1936* **Right.** *In 1933 delegates to the Co-operative Commonwealth Federation party convention put together an election platform called the "Regina Manifesto." The Manifesto called for the government to nationalize many essential services and intervene in other areas of the economy. CCF leader Woodsworth blames unregulated capitalism for the problems associated with the Depression.* Winnipeg Free Press, *8 May 1936*

THE OCTOPUS
Will its tentacles get a grip on Canada?

Germany and Italy used their consulates to promote nazi and fascist ideas among German and Italian immigrants to Canada. Small native fascist parties also emerged across Canada among people attracted by the parties' anti-Semitic and anti-communist stances and the low unemployment levels in Germany and Italy. The Monetary Times, *Montreal, 14 Nov 1936*

STEPPING OUT
The Export Trade of Canadian Mining Products is Flourishing.

One bright spot in the Canadian economy was the mining industry. As the nations of the world began to rearm, demand for Canadian minerals increased. It would be 1938 before poor crops in other parts of the world allowed Canada to sell its surplus wheat. Winnipeg Free Press, 21 Apr 1936

"ONE IS SUFFICIENT"

PREMIER KING: "Now here's a dog that is a dog!" JACK CANUCK: "Yes! but what do I want with him? I have a good English bulldog already!"

THE CITY SLICKER

Left. In 1936 Prime Minister King amended the Bank of Canada Act to ensure government control of the central bank. The legislation also provided for bilingual currency. Conservative leader Bennett vehemently opposed the latter, stating that it would "destroy the fabric of the nation." The Evening Telegram, *Toronto, 27 June 1936* **Right.** *Canadian magazines had a hard time competing with their American rivals, which had access to a market more than ten times as large and were tax-free to boot.* The Hamilton Spectator, *5 Feb 1936*

THE STAR BOARDER

OH CANADA!

Left. The high government debt and high interest on the debt imposed a serious burden on taxpayers. The Vancouver Daily Province, *6 Feb 1936* **Right.** *In 1936 Canada was completely unprepared for war. The few guns it did possess were obsolete; it did not have a single modern anti-aircraft gun or tank; and its 25 aircraft were useless except for training purposes. Canada depended on Britain and the United States for protection without sharing any of the costs.* The Hamilton Spectator, *20 Oct 1936*

GOOD FRIENDS MEET AGAIN
... the costumes have changed, but not the hearts.

In 1936 a national memorial was unveiled at Vimy Ridge in France to honour all Canadians who fought for their country in the First World War, and in particular the almost 67,000 who lost their lives. The design, which came to sculptor Walter Allward in a dream, features two pylons which symbolize the Canadian and French forces. La Patrie Dimanche, *Montreal, 26 July 1936*

SUCH FUNNY BUSINESS WON'T WORK

Alberta premier William Aberhart showed little tolerance for criticism of his Social Credit government. In January 1936 he told his followers that reporters were a nuisance and that his government must control the press. The press refused to be intimidated by Aberhart. Winnipeg Free Press, 7 Jan 1936

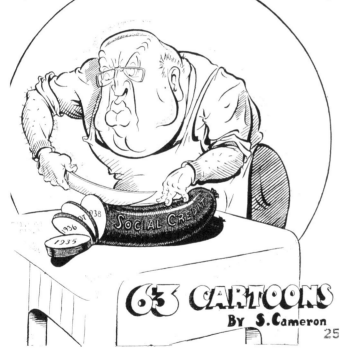

No Matter How Thin You Slice It—,

63 CARTOONS
By S.Cameron
25

CHÂTEAUX DE CARTES
Histoire sans parôles

Left. *By far the most cutting anti-Social Credit cartoons were drawn by a Calgary cartoonist. The above cartoon was on the front cover of a popular collection entitled "No Matter How Thin You Slice It."* Calgary Herald, 1937 **Right.** HOUSE OF CARDS. *Story without words. [tr.] Between 1937 and 1941 King used federal powers to disallow nine pieces of financial legislation passed by Aberhart's Social Credit government in Alberta.* La Presse, Montreal, 21 Aug 1937

JUST A FRIENDLY LITTLE GAME — OH YEAH!

In addition to low prices for wheat, farmers had to deal with wind, drought, rust and grasshoppers. Over a quarter of a million farmers migrated from the southern Prairies to less arid lands farther north, to the cities or to the United States. Winnipeg Free Press, *25 June 1937*

LA GRAND MENACE
À quoi bon le Congrès de la langue française si John Bull veut nos noyer par l'immigration intensive.

LA FEMME À BARBE
La vieille p...oule se farde

Left. THE GREAT THREAT. *What good is the French language Congress if John Bull wants to swamp us with intensive immigration.* [tr.] *Many people in Quebec looked unfavourably on immigration as most new arrivals spoke or adopted the English language. The cartoonist, like many French Canadians, fears for the survival of the French language and culture. La Nation, Quebec, 25 Mar 1937* **Right.** THE BEARDED WOMAN. *The old tart puts on her makeup.* [tr.] *Many young, unemployed university graduates and others joined nationalist societies that were anti-English, antitrust and often anti-Semitic. They gloried in the French Canadian "race" and favoured separatism. The cartoonist takes a stand against such groups. Le Jour, Montreal, 16 Oct 1937*

THE MONSTER'S BREEDING GROUND.

SONGE D'UN SOIR D'HIVER
Pour lui comme pour bien d'autres, "la crise l'a pas voulu."

*Left. The poverty and squalor found in city slums were seen as the cause of crime and other social ills. The death rate increased during the Depression as people who could not afford medical care delayed seeing a doctor as long as possible. Winnipeg Free Press, 30 Mar 1937 **Right.** DREAM OF A WINTER EVENING. For him, as for many others, life is passing him by. [tr.] For many young people the Depression represented lost years. Unable to find work, they had to postpone plans for marriage, a family and a home of their own. Le Siffleux, Montreal, 13 Feb 1937*

THE RECEPTION COMMITTEE
"If only the animal were not hungry."

THE TIE THAT BINDS OUR FAR-FLUNG EMPIRE
An object-lesson to the world, and in particular to certain nations
who cast covetous eyes on vital parts of the world's greatest Empire.

Left. Prime Minister Bennett called for increased immigration. The newcomers would need goods and services and housing, and some had the skills needed to start new businesses in Canada. While some people supported the idea, most opposed immigration at a time of high unemployment. One group caught in the controversy were Jewish refugees seeking to escape discrimination in Europe. Canada refused to change its restrictive immigration policies to accommodate them. The Monetary Times, *Toronto, 30 Jan 1937* **Right.** *In 1937 Prime Minister King travelled to London to attend the coronation of King George VI, a ceremony that strengthened Canada's ties to the Empire.* The Montreal Daily Star, *8 May 1937*

LET'S SEE NOW – WHERE'S THAT MIDDLE COURSE

HITLER–"I JUST HATE WAR"

Left. *Pacifists wanted to spend as little as possible on national defence, which they feared would draw Canada into an Imperial war. Others wanted Canada to be ready to assist if the need arose.* The Vancouver Sun, *16 Feb 1937*
Right. *In 1937 Mackenzie King visited Germany. He was completely taken in by Hitler's statements that he opposed war. King did warn Hitler that if any part of the Commonwealth were threatened all the Dominions would come to its aid.* The Standard, *Montreal, 17 July 1937*

RÉSULTAT DE LA CONFÉRENCE IMPÉRIALE
Les armements—La conscription—La guerre!

THE TWO WORLDS

RESULT OF THE IMPERIAL CONFERENCE: Armaments–conscription–war! [tr.] Quebeckers were prepared to defend themselves at home but not to risk their lives on foreign soil. King was well aware of their opposition to conscription and the production of armaments for Imperial defence. At the 1937 Imperial Conference in London he rejected all proposals of collective security. L'Idée Ouvrière, Saint Hyacinthe, 29 May 1937 **Right.** *By the end of 1937 it was becoming increasingly clear to Britain, Canada and the United States that world peace was threatened by three major dictatorships. Winnipeg Free Press, 20 Nov 1937*

MISS CANADA: "HERE LIES YOUR POWER"

Left. Miss Canada reminds women to use the power of the franchise to improve their lives. Reason, *Toronto, 23 Feb 1938* **Right.** *In 1938 few native people had the right to vote as they would have to give up their status under the Indian Act to do so. Both the potential voter and the stereotypical native are baffled by the promises of the various parties.* The Leader-Post, *Regina, 25 May 1938*

LIGHTING THE BOOK

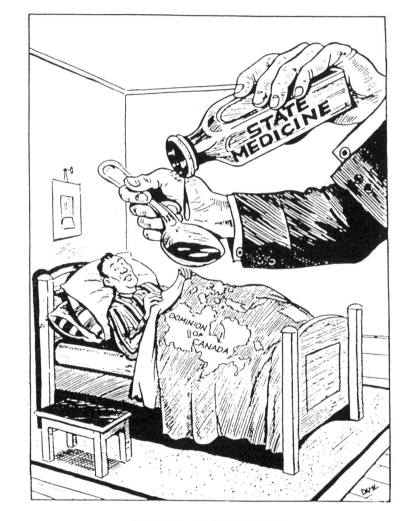

IT STILL IS NECESSARY!

Left. *The federal government was concerned about rebuilding the population after the losses of the First World War. Veneral diseases were a serious concern. In 1938 the government finally decided to work with the provinces and volunteer groups on a program of public education.* The Vancouver Daily Province, *2 Feb 1938* **Right.** *The Depression greatly increased the problems associated with Canada's health care system. The need for health care increased at a time when more and more people could not afford it. Politicians, among them many doctors, were beginning to debate the need for a government-run medical system.* Reason, *Toronto, 10 Mar 1938*

IN THE NAME OF FREEDOM!

LE CHARMEUR DE SERPENTS

*Left. When King repealed Section 98 of the Criminal Code, which dealt with communist activity in Canada, Premier Duplessis of Quebec replaced it with the Padlock Law. The new law made it illegal to use a house or hall "to propagate communism or bolshevism." Because the term "communism" was not defined, the law was used against moderate socialist or liberal groups. The Toronto Daily Star, 12 Jan 1938 **Right.** THE SNAKE CHARMER. [tr.] People opposed to the Quebec Loi du Cadenas, or Padlock Law, accused it of being fascist in nature and a clear violation of civil liberties. En Avant!, Saint-Hyacinthe, 16 Sep 1938*

"THE MICAWBER GOVERNMENT"

Left. *The cartoonist compares Prime Minister King to a character in Charles Dickens' novel* David Copperfield, *who had little money but a lot of optimism and was always sure that "something would turn up." King's optimism was of little consolation to the unemployed.* The Vancouver Sun, *5 May 1938*
Right. *Fascists believed that a strong authoritarian government would save Canada from swamping in a sea of depression and economic stagnation.* Le Fasciste Canadien, *Montreal, June 1938*

DRIVER: "WHY NOT LIGHTEN THE LOAD?"

In 1938 the King government passed an act designed to encourage the building of homes. It also consciously gave up the idea of a balanced budget and decided to spend money to stimulate economic recovery. The Conservative cartoonist suggests that lower taxes would do more than government incentives to stimulate business and restore prosperity. Saturday Night, *Toronto, 18 June 1938*

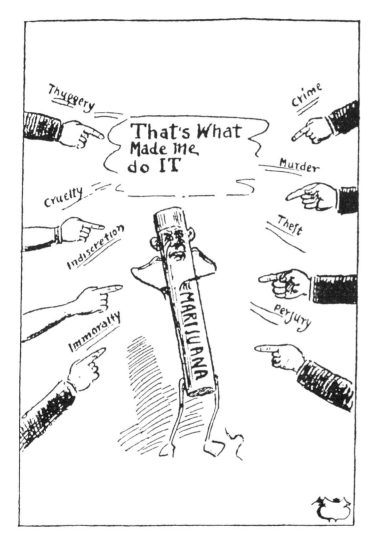

THE SCAPEGOAT

INTERESTING DEDUCTION, MY DEAR WATSON!

Left. Many criminal activities were attributed to illegal drug use. Canada was the first western nation to prohibit the use of opium. Laws against drugs such as marijuana soon followed. The Evening Telegram, *Toronto, 15 Aug 1938* **Right.** *While horse racing was legal, and the winners of the illegal Irish sweepstakes were front page news, bingo players were harassed for gambling.* The Toronto Daily Star, *27 Oct 1938*

RIBALD SUGGESTION FOR CANADIAN FLAG

A BADLY WEAKENED DYKE

Left. Conservatives, including Tommy Church, opposed a motion calling for a distinctive Canadian flag to replace the Union Jack. The cartoonist has incorporated the perennial fight over provincial rights into his suggested design. The Vancouver Daily Province, *26 Feb 1938* **Right.** *Japan's invasion of China in 1937 resulted in an increase in anti-Japanese sentiment in British Columbia. In 1938 King negotiated an agreement with Japan to limit immigration from Japan to 150 individuals per year.* The Vancouver Daily Province, *22 Feb 1938*

FIN D'ANNÉE SCOLAIRE
Va, mon petit... Tu es préparé à continuer la tâche de tes Pères!

CAPITALISM'S ALTERNATIVES

Left. *END OF THE SCHOOL YEAR. Go, my little one. You are ready to carry on the work of your fathers. [tr.] English Canadians dominated the top and middle positions in business and industry, while most French Canadians remained "hewers of wood and drawers of water." Some people blamed this situation on the church-controlled schools and colleges, which had not kept pace with the times.* Le Jour, *Montreal, 14 May 1938* **Right.** *Socialists blamed unemployment, crime, hunger and war on capitalism, which went through a cycle of booms and busts.* The Federationist, *Vancouver, 28 Apr 1938*

LES GANGSTERS PEUVENT VENIR!
Baptiste Canayen se sent à présent plus brave.

Left. King believed that Canada had a special role to play in uniting Britain and the United States in friendship, trade and defence. Canada depended on both Britain and the United States for defence, and good relations with both were very much in the national interest. The Canadian Liberal Monthly, *Ottawa, Nov 1938*
Right. LET THE GANGSTERS COME! Baptiste feels a lot braver now. *[tr.] In August 1938 American president Roosevelt made a commitment to come to the aid of Canada if it were threatened "by any other empire." The promise was aimed at the expansionist policies of Hitler, Mussolini and Hirohito (right). Although Roosevelt was taking responsibility for Canada's defence, King was pleased rather than embarrassed.* Le Jour, *Montreal, 27 Aug 1938*

NATIONAL NIGHTMARE

TRYING TO PLEASE BOTH.

*Left. In September 1938 Hitler pushed the world close to war in a dispute over Czechoslovakia. Canada suddenly realized that its inadequate armed forces left it vulnerable to attack. In December 1938 the cabinet increased the defence budget from 35 million to 60 million dollars. Half of the budget was allotted to the air force, as the air force was thought to be less likely to involve Canada in foreign wars. The Hamilton Spectator, 8 Feb 1939 **Right.** Hitler's invasion of Czechoslovakia in March 1939 made a European war much more likely. To please the imperialists King told Parliament that Canada would defend Britain if Britain were attacked. To pacify the nationalists he promised that there would be no conscription for overseas service. The Gazette, Montreal, 24 Apr 1939*

ROW, ROW, ROW YOUR BOAT GENTLY DOWN THE STREAM...

LEFT ON THE DOORSTEP

Left. In 1937 a royal commission on Dominion–provincial relations was appointed to consider the allocation of federal and provincial powers. One point in contention was which level of government should have control over unemployment insurance. The report was delivered but shelved until after the war. The Hamilton Spectator, 26 July 1939 **Right.** *After nearly a decade of high unemployment, the different levels of government were still fighting over which one was responsible for the problem. The Gazette, Montreal, 6 Mar 1939*

CANADIAN CRUSADE

"LO, THE POOR INDIAN ..."

Left. *While treatment for tuberculosis, influenza, bronchitis, pneumonia and other diseases was improving, the death rate for cancer and heart disease was increasing.* The Gazette, *Montreal, 10 Mar 1939* **Right.** *The article which accompanied this cartoon commented on the exploitation of native artisans who received very little for their work while others prospered from it.* The Halifax Herald, *14 Feb 1939*

THE NEXT STEP?

Left. This cartoon summarizes Hitler's domestic and foreign policy up to 1939 and predicts that his next step will lead to his downfall. Unfortunately the democracies were not nearly as well prepared for war as the cartoon would suggest. The Halifax Herald, *21 Mar 1939* **Right.** *King George VI and Queen Elizabeth cemented Canadian support for Britain when they visited Canada in May and June of 1939. Their visit to the United States did the same for Anglo–American relations.* The Country Guide and Nor-West Farmer, *Winnipeg, July 1939*

CAN WE AFFORD NOT TO RECEIVE SOME OF THEM?　　　**WAITING FOR THEIR CUE**

Left. Many European refugees were well educated and had skills that would have been useful in Canada. Although Canada had a population of under 11 million, many Canadians opposed increased immigration because of continued high unemployment levels and anti-Semitic feelings. The Windsor Daily Star, *1 Aug 1939*
Right. This cartoon was published on September 1, 1939, the day Hitler invaded Poland. Britain declared war on September 3, and Canada declared war on September 10. The Halifax Herald, *1 Sep 1939*

GOING TO BE A HORNETS' NEST FOR SOMEBODY

Left. *The Canadian army had suffered such high casualties in the First World War that conscription became necessary. King wanted to avoid such a scenario in the Second World War. When Britain asked Canada to train a vastly enlarged air force he jumped at the chance. The Commonwealth Air Training Plan would allow Canada to make an important contribution to the war with far fewer total casualties.* The Toronto Daily Star, *11 Oct 1939* **Right.** *Union Nationale leader Maurice Duplessis feared that the war and the War Measures Act would strengthen the federal government and threaten provincial autonomy. He called a provincial election for October 25. Fearing that a Union Nationale victory would signal Quebec's opposition to the war, King helped elect a Liberal government.* En Avant!, *Saint-Hyacinthe, 20 Oct 1939*

DESCENDANT D'UNE RACE FIÈRE QUE PRÉFÈRES-TU?
LA LIBERTÉ?...   ...LA SERVITUDE?

DESCENDANT OF A PROUD RACE, WHICH DO YOU PREFER? LIBERTY? SERVITUDE? Hitler's treatment of the Catholic church in Germany and Austria and his non-aggression treaty with the Soviet Union destroyed much of the remaining fascist sympathy within Canada. A. Lemay, Que Préfères-Tu?, Ministère des Services Nationaux de Guerre, *Ottawa, 1940*

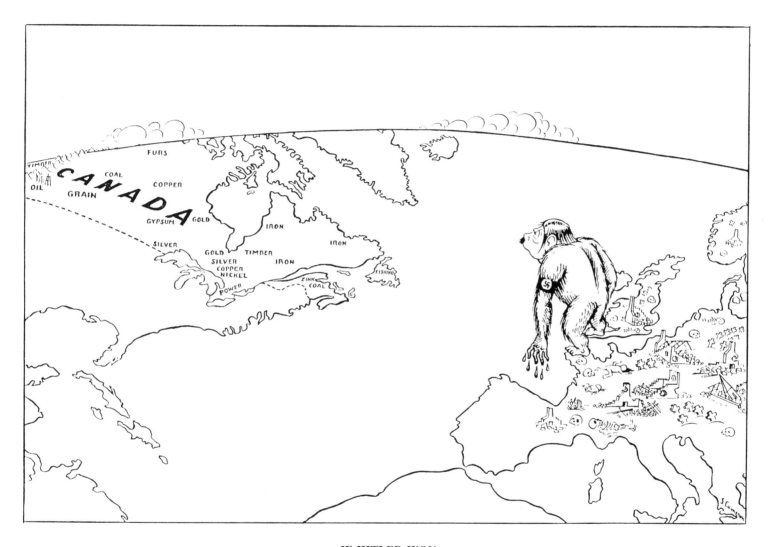

IF HITLER WON

The spectacular success of Hitler's invasion of Belgium, the Netherlands, Luxembourg and France in May and June of 1940 suddenly made Canada Britain's leading ally. King realized that if Britain were defeated Hitler might turn his attention to Canada and its largely unexploited resources. He immediately increased war production and recruitment for the armed forces and imposed conscription for home defence. The Calgary Herald, *23 May 1940*

THE ENEMY ON THE HOME FRONT

REALLY, THIS IS SO SUDDEN

Left. During the First World War businessmen became rich while many of the most promising young men in the country risked their lives at sea and in Europe. In 1939 the government established the Wartime Prices and Trade Board to try to prevent hoarding and profiteering and conserve civilian supplies. In 1941 a price ceiling was approved. The Halifax Herald, *10 Jan 1940* **Right.** *In the 1939 fall election the provincial Liberal party promised women the vote if they were elected. The Liberals defeated the Union Nationale under Maurice Duplessis and on April 25, 1940, women in Quebec were given the vote and the right to hold provincial office.* The Toronto Daily Star, *22 Feb 1940*

RIGHT ON THE JOB

OUR JOB NOW

Left. In September 1939 civil rights were suspended under the War Measures Act. The government planned to intern fascists, nazis, communists and other suspected subversives. After Germany's victories in Europe in May 1940 many fascist leaders were interned for the rest of the war. This was one Ottawa action that Ontario premier "Mitch" Hepburn supported. The Toronto Daily Star, *13 June 1940* **Right.** *After the events of May and June 1940 Canada went all out to help Britain, taking the place of a fallen France.* The Leader-Post, *Regina, 3 July 1940*

AN OTTAWA LULLABY

I love little Kitty, Her coat is so warm,
And if I don't tease her, She'll do me no harm.

SO MUCH IN COMMON

Left. Many Canadians opposed Japan's expansionist policies and urged Prime Minister King to boycott Japanese imports and place an embargo on goods going to Japan. King did not want to risk provoking retaliation by Japan. The Evening Telegram, *Toronto, 4 Oct 1940* **Right.** *In August 1940 King agreed to American president Roosevelt's proposal for a Permanent Joint Board of Defence. The Ogdensburg agreement bound Canada to a continental defence system dominated by the United States. This short meeting between the two men marked Canada's shift from the British to the American sphere of influence.* Winnipeg Free Press, *20 Aug 1940*

THE ENGAGEMENT RING

FORGING ANOTHER LINK

Left. Canada was purchasing more goods from the United States than it was selling, and its trade deficit was growing. In April Prime Minister King made a special visit to Hyde Park, the president's country house on the Hudson River. The Hyde Park Declaration stated that "each country should provide the other with the defence articles which it is best able to produce." Trade began to flow in both directions. The Calgary Herald, 24 April 1941 **Right.** Many Americans had settled in Alberta. This link, and the western culture Albertans shared with their American neighbours, helped account for the success of the Calgary Stampede in bringing the two nations together. The Calgary Herald, 12 July 1941

Hold on my little one, Baptiste has had his share. Here is yours!!! [tr.] French Canadians were seriously underrepresented in senior civil service positions. With relatively little power in Ottawa, they opposed any loss of provincial power to the federal government. Some wondered why they should be fighting for the liberty of Europeans when liberty was denied them at home. La Terre de Chez Nous, *Montreal, 8 Jan 1941*

DANS UN PAYS BILINGUE
Pourquoi pas du bilinguisme des deux côtés du guichet?

"HEROES ARE MADE — "

Left. IN A BILINGUAL COUNTRY. *Why not have bilingualism on both sides of the wicket? [tr.] Linguistic grievances seem to intensify in Canada in wartime. During the First World War bilingual rights in Ontario were a matter of concern. During the Second World War problems arose over linguistic practices in the workplace in such places as Montreal and Ottawa.* Chez Nous, Montreal, 6 Oct 1941 **Right.** *Germany and the Soviet Union had signed a non-aggression pact in 1939, but in 1941 Hitler invaded the Soviet Union. Stalin now became a hero fighting on the side of the Allies. The adjustment was difficult for many Canadians and for this cartoonist.* The Calgary Herald, 24 June 1941

"HELL HATH NO FURY"

Left. Women in Ontario would not gain the right to sit on juries until 1952; those in Quebec would wait until 1971. In 1972 the federal government would abolish discrimination against female jurors in criminal cases. The Windsor Daily Star, *25 Mar 1941* **Right**. *This Quebec cartoon repeats the theme that big business controlled both the Liberal and the Conservative parties*. La Voix du Peuple, *Montreal, 14 June 1941*

THREE MEN IN A BOAT

THE EMPIRE PHALANX

Left. *Canada very much wanted the United States to enter the war on Britain's side. Many cartoons such as this one tried to discredit the isolationists' position or shame the United States into action.* The Gazette, *Montreal, 12 Feb 1941* **Right.** *As in the First World War, Britain's former colonies willingly sent troops to her defence.* The Halifax Herald, *24 May 1941*

CANADIAN SURPRISE

In 1941 Britain asked Canada to send troops to reinforce the British colony of Hong Kong against a threatened Japanese invasion. King gladly sent two ill-prepared battalions, the Royal Rifles and the Winnipeg Grenadiers, from Vancouver on October 27. The pride and optimism of Canadians is revealed in this Winnipeg cartoon. British prime minister Churchill failed to mention to King his belief that if Japan went to war "there is not the faintest chance of holding Hong Kong."
Winnipeg Free Press, *18 Nov 1941*

NOS CONSCRIPTIONNISTES SONT MENAÇANTS

OUR CONSCRIPTIONISTS ARE THREATENING. This cartoon clearly portrays the attitude of Quebec toward conscription. King was kept well informed by his Quebec colleagues of the threat conscription posed to national unity. L'Action Catholique, *Quebec, 25 Nov 1941*

NERO WASN'T THE ONLY KING WHO FIDDLED

Left. *In order to avoid a split within his party and in the country, King held a plebiscite asking Canadians to release the government from its election pledge not to introduce conscription for overseas service.* The Vancouver Daily Province, *29 Jan 1942* **Right.** THE RESULT OF THE PLEBISCITE. *The result of the plebiscite was a blow to national unity. French-speaking Canadians voted overwhelmingly against conscription while English-speaking Canadians voted just as strongly in favour. French Canadians had agreed to war in 1939 on the clear condition that conscription for overseas service would never be introduced.* La Boussole, Montreal, 2 May 1942

THE UNITED NATIONS

A PROBLEM IN DIVISION

PRENEZ! PRENEZ! MESSIEURS

Upper left. Japan's attack on Pearl Harbour brought an abrupt end to American isolationism. King saw Canada as the linchpin uniting the efforts of the United States and Britain. Winnipeg Free Press, *10 Jan 1942* **Lower left.** *By 1942 manpower was in short supply. The government organized the National Selective Service to allocate scarce manpower to essential services.* Saturday Night, Toronto, *11 July 1942* **Right.** TAKE! TAKE! GENTLEMEN. *Foreign investment and foreign ownership were important issues in Quebec.* L'Union, Montreal, *30 Apr 1942*

"STRATEGIC WITHDRAWAL TO PREPARED POSITIONS"   **LET CANADA ANSWER *THIS***

Left. *Soon after Japan bombed Pearl Harbour in December 1941, thousands of Japanese Canadians were forcibly removed from their homes along the coast of British Columbia and sent to work camps or detention camps in the interior of BC. Some were sent outside the province. All lost their possessions. Ironically, no person of Japanese ancestry had been charged with any act of sabotage or disloyalty during the war.* The Toronto Daily Star, *21 Jan 1942* **Right.** *The battle at Hong Kong resulted in the death of 290 Canadians. Nearly as many died in prisoner-of-war or work camps from malnutrition, disease and lack of medical treatment. The 1,418 members of the Canadian force who survived the war suffered physically and mentally from their years of captivity.* The Halifax Herald, *11 Mar 1942*

"THE HUN IS AT THE GATE!"

THOSE CIRCLES UNDER HIS EYES

Left. After Japan's attack on Pearl Harbour, the United States transferred the bulk of its fleet to the Pacific. Britain and Canada now shared escort duty to protect the men and materials convoyed across the North Atlantic. The Halifax Herald, *14 Jan 1942* **Right.** *The Royal Canadian Air Force and Britain's Royal Air Force played a major role in bombing German targets and reducing Hitler's military effectiveness. By 1945 Canadians would make up a quarter of the air crew in the British Bomber Command.* The Montreal Daily Star, *10 June 1942*

TEMPERING THE SPEARHEAD

THE MEN WHO BLAZED THE WAY

Left. In the summer of 1942 Canada participated in a raid on the French port of Dieppe, which was held by the German army. This cartoon reflects Canadian optimism and desire for action. The Toronto Daily Star, *20 Aug 1942* **Right.** *The mainly Canadian attack on Dieppe was a failure. The direct frontal assault on a well-defended city lacked both a preliminary naval or air bombardment and the element of surprise. The Halifax Herald, 25 Aug 1942*

Bert Grassick

TOO BAD WE DON'T HAVE MORE OF THAT UNITY ON THE HOME FRONT

Canadian soldiers faced fierce German resistance at Dieppe and suffered a major defeat. The cartoonist has focused on the raid as a cause that united Canadians from different parts of the country. The Financial Post, *Toronto, 5 Sep 1942*

PUT HIM WHERE HE BELONGS

OPEN WIDE THE GATES

Left. *The war demonstrated the immense power of government to increase industrial production. Many people, like the cartoonist, believed that the power of government should be harnessed after the war to end such things as unemployment and racial hatred.* Manitoba Commonwealth, *Winnipeg, 16 Apr 1943*
Right. *The attitude of Canadians toward immigration was starting to change. Many people believed that a sparsely populated country such as Canada should be able to find room for the victims of Nazi policies.* Manitoba Commonwealth, *Winnipeg, 28 May 1943*

—Cartoon by Grassick

"...an end must be found to Britain
and the U. S. making all decisions."

WAR WORKER, 1943

Left. *For years Prime Minister King had avoided consulting Britain about foreign policy and military strategy as he feared that such consultation would lead to future military commitments. He had also avoided sending representatives to the Supreme War Council. This lack of representation on the council angered many Canadians, who felt that Canada's significant contribution to the war effort had earned it a share in making related decisions.* Maclean's Magazine, *Toronto, 15 Aug 1943* **Right.** *In 1943 the federal government launched a major campaign to increase the number of women in the work force and in the armed forces. Many were already working on farms, and others were quick to seize opportunities in the service sector, manufacturing, trade and commerce, transportation, construction and the armed forces. "Rosie the Riveter" became a popular icon.* The Winnipeg Tribune, *6 Sep 1943*

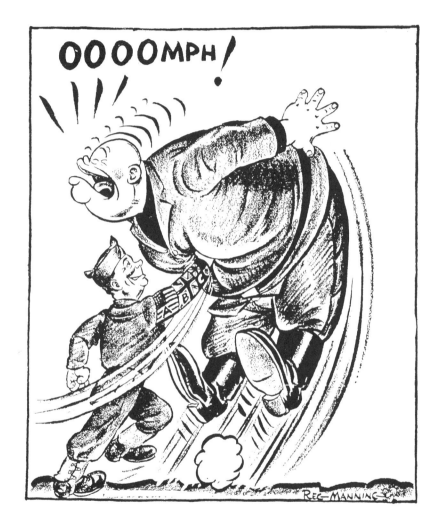

THE RELENTLESS STRUGGLE

'SOFT UNDERBELLY OF EUROPE'

Left. During the first few years of the war the Royal Canadian Navy lacked the experience and equipment needed to adequately protect convoys in the Atlantic. In 1942 German submarines were able to penetrate the St. Lawrence River and sink more than 20 ships. Losses in the "Battle of the Atlantic" were heavy until May 1943, when an increase in the escort fleet and the acquisition of long-range bombers turned the tide. The Winnipeg Tribune, *2 July 1943* **Right.** *In July 1943 the Canadian army joined the British and Americans in attacking Mussolini's troops in Sicily and southern Italy.* The Vancouver News-Herald, *19 July 1943*

Left. THE YOUNG WONDER. YESTERDAY A CHILD... TODAY A COLOSSUS! [tr.] Before 1940 Canada had a very small arms industry and relied on other countries for its military equipment. Hitler's success in the summer of 1940 meant that Canada had to quickly start producing war materials on a large scale. La Patrie, Montreal, 19 Apr 1943 **Right.** THE MOST HANDSOME "YOUTH" OF THE CENTURY. He has developed so quickly and so well that the world is amazed. [tr.] The increase in Canada's military and industrial power during the Second World War greatly increased Canada's status and power as a nation. La Patrie, Montreal, 24 July 1943

OUR STRONG RIGHT ARM   **RENDERING FINE SERVICE**

Left. Merchant seamen played a vital, and hazardous, role in supplying food and manufactured goods to civilians and to the armed forces in Europe. One man in 10 lost his life, compared to one in 16 in the air force, one in 32 in the army and one in 41 in the navy. The Montreal Daily Star, 10 June 1943 **Right.** *In 1943 and 1944 the federal government encouraged women to join the armed forces. Women took over many of the administrative tasks in order to free more men to fight at the front. The Halifax Herald, 28 Aug 1943*

THE HURDLE

SIDE-SHOW

Left. Prime Minister King was a master at balancing English Canada's demand for conscription with Quebec's strong opposition to such a policy. The Gazette, *Montreal, 22 Feb 1943* **Right.** *At one point in 1943 the Co-operative Commonwealth Federation (CCF) polled slightly ahead of the Liberals and Progressive Conservatives. Its popularity concerned the old parties, which attacked it at every opportunity.* The Gazette, *Montreal, 30 Nov 1943*

"MAKE THIS YOUR CANADA"

Critics of the Co-operative Commonwealth Federation predicted that the Canadian economy would be strangled by government controls under a socialist government. They also attacked many of the ideas generated by left-wing intellectuals. The Winnipeg Free Press, *18 Feb 1944*

Bert Grassick

MAY COME IN HANDY

The CCF defeat of the Liberals in Saskatchewan in June 1944 helped encourage King to implement some of the ideas of the welfare state. Family allowances were attractive as they could be implemented in time for the approaching federal election and would reduce the inflationary demands of unions for pay increases. The money would be placed in the hands of people who would spend it on necessities, stimulating the postwar economy. Financial Post, *Toronto, 1 July 1944*

NOTHING BUT TROUBLE AHEAD

Canadians played a major role in the defeat of Hitler. The navy transported supplies to Russia via Murmansk, the air force helped bomb Germany, and the army played an important role in Italy and France. Winnipeg Free Press, *2 Jun 1944*

TRIPES À LA MODE DE CAEN

TRIPE, CAEN STYLE. "Tripes à la mode de Caen" is a dish made from the lining of beef stomach and served in Caen, Normandy. The cartoon refers to the successful Canadian, American and British landings on the beaches of Normandy on D-Day, June 6, 1944. Le Canada, *Montreal, 8 Jun 1944*

QUAND LA DROITE VAUT LA GAUCHE

WHEN THE RIGHT IS AS GOOD AS THE LEFT. [tr.] The Allied Air Force acted as a powerful second front against Germany. Canadian flyers played a part in air raids on German cities and industrial targets. They also bombed railways and German defences in France prior to the Allied invasion of Normandy on D-Day, June 6, 1944. Le Canada, *Montreal, 17 June 1944*

THE DUTCH MILL GRINDS ON

Left. The grindstone is an apt analogy for the Canadian army's slow but steady advance in Holland. The Montreal Daily Star, *31 Oct 1944* **Right.** *Canada learned a lot from the First World War about the need to control inflation and reduce profiteering. The government instituted wage and price controls, used income taxes to pay most of the cost of the war, and sold bonds. It also controlled manpower, consumer credit, and the production, distribution, and consumption of goods. The system worked but people were concerned about what would happen when the controls were removed.* Le Jour, *Montreal, 2 Sep 1944*

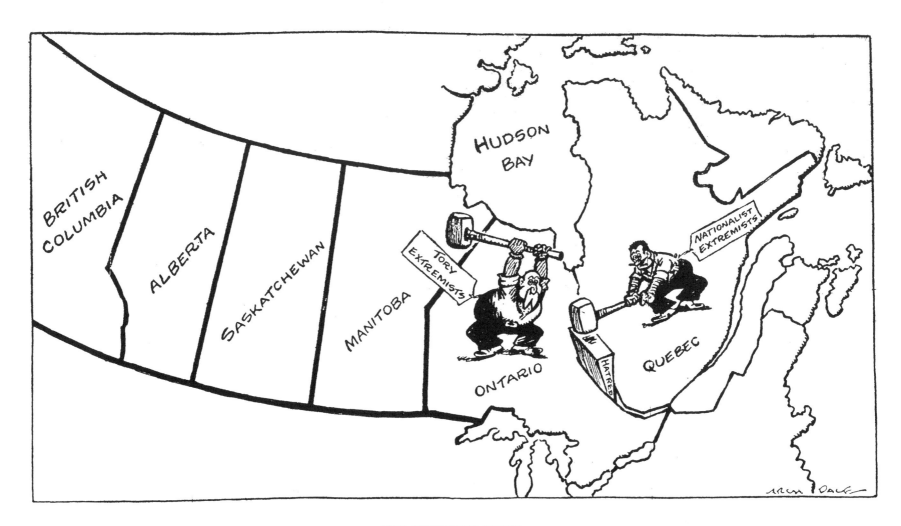

THE WRECKING CREW

The invasion of Italy in 1943 and France in 1944 brought heavy losses to the Canadian army. The Progressive Conservative Party (the Tories) demanded that the government make men allotted to home defence available for overseas service. Extreme antiwar, anticonscriptionist rhetoric was unleashed by a provincial election in Quebec. Maritimers were upset by this cartoon because their provinces were drawn badly and not named at all. Winnipeg Free Press, 5 Aug 1944

RIGHT UNDER HIS NOSE

THE BLUSHING BRIDEGROOM

Left. *"Zombie" was a slang term for Canadians who had been conscripted but who refused to serve overseas. By 1944 they were no longer needed for home defence. The cartoonist suggests that they should be used to reduce manpower shortages in industry and agriculture.* The Gazette, *Toronto, 14 June 1944*
Right. *The Minister of Defence was convinced that conscription must replace voluntary enlistment. Faced with overwhelming pressure from English Canada, Prime Minister King finally relented. Instead of imposing all-out conscription, the government agreed to send just 16,000 of the 68,000 home defence army overseas.* The Gazette, *Montreal, 2 Dec 1944*

Bert Grassick

... THERE IS ALWAYS A CRITICAL INTERVAL

MORTE LA BÊTE, MORT LE VENIN

Left. *During the war King did a masterful job of balancing the pro- and anticonscriptionist forces in the interest of national unity, and avoided the near-fatal divisions caused by conscription in the First World War.* Maclean's Magazine, *Toronto, 1 Jan 1945* **Right.** THE BEAST IS DEAD, THE VENOM STAUNCHED. *After almost six years of war and the recent revelations of Nazi death camps, most people would have agreed with the artist's assessment of Adolf Hitler.* La Presse, *Montreal, 2 May 1945*

LES CANAYENS SONT LLA! LAPALME

LE VRAI HÉROS DU 24 JUIN... ON LE VERRA SUR LE PARCOURS DE LA PROCESSION

ECONOMIC PLANNING? ENTIRELY TOO RADICAL! IT WOULD KILL INITIATIVE AND ENTERPRISE! CUT DOWN PROFITS TOO!.....HRRRMPH! A CERTAIN AMOUNT OF UNEMPLOYMENT IS NECESSARY, SIR! GOOD FOR 'EM! KEEPS 'EM ON THEIR TOES! — AND IN THEIR PLACE!

WAR PROFITS

BACK TO SCARCITY & DEPRESSION

STEPHEN

Upper left. THE CANADIANS ARE THERE! *Canadians had a lot to be proud of at the end of the war in Europe. Over a million men and women had served in the armed forces and 42,000 had given their lives.* Le Canada, *Montreal, 8 May 1945* **Lower left.** THE TRUE HERO OF JUNE 24 WILL BE SEEN ON THE PARADE ROUTE. *St. Jean Baptiste is the patron saint of Quebec. The cartoonist suggests that the veteran who served his country during the war would be the true hero at the St. Jean Baptiste Day parade on June 24.* Le Canada, *Montreal, 23 June 1945* **Right.** *The cartoonist recalls the consequences of an unplanned economy during the Depression of the 1930s.* Saskatchewan Commonwealth, Regina, *15 Aug 1945*

DON'T MAKE HIM AN INVALID

BABY KISSING TIME

*Left. By 1943 the government was already preparing for postwar reconstruction and rehabilitation. The Marsh Report called for a major program of social security including medical care, family allowances, disability pensions and old age pensions. The idea became more and more popular as the end of the war approached, but some felt it was "pie in the sky" and far too costly. The Globe and Mail, Toronto, 10 Mar 1945 **Right.** The promise of family allowance cheques played an important role in the election of Mackenzie King in 1945. The Gazette, Montreal, 6 June 1945*

CANADA SALUTES YOU!

This cartoon, published on the first anniversary of the Normandy invasion, reminds Canadians of the price paid for victory. The Montreal Daily Star, *June 6, 1945*

THEY "GET TOGETHER" IN ONE RESPECT

Left. A strike at the Ford plant in Windsor, Ontario, inspired this cartoon. An arbitration award determined that all members of the bargaining unit would have union dues deducted from their cheques but that no one would be required to join the union. This ruling later became known as the Rand formula. The Toronto Daily Star, *13 Dec 1945* **Right.** *At the end of the war the government planned to deport 10,000 people of Japanese ancestry who had declared under duress their wish to return to Japan. Most, including the stereotypical applicant in this cartoon, later changed their minds.* The Daily Colonist, Victoria, *30 Dec 1945*

ANTI-LABOR
ANTI-SEMITISM
ANTI-CATHOLICISM
WHITE SUPREMA

MADE IN GERMANY

PREJUDICE
DISCRIMINATION
IGNORANCE
EXPLOITATION
HATRED

COURTESY LABOR REPORT

THE BRIDGE OF FASCISM

ATOMIC ENERGY

HOW TO GET THE GENIE BACK IN THE BOTTLE?

Left. The Nazi death camps showed the world the consequences of fascist values. At the end of the war many people were determined to eliminate such ideas from our society. The Gazette, Glace Bay, NS, 20 Aug 1945 ***Right.*** *Canada and Britain had played a role in helping the United States to produce the atomic bombs used to knock Japan out of the war. King, British prime minister Atlee and US president Truman ponder the potential destructive power of atomic energy. The Gazette,* Montreal, 12 Nov 1945

PLACE CARD

"Canada has made her position very clearly known." — W. L. M. King

Canadians felt that they had earned a place at the peace table and a special place in the United Nations. The Montreal Daily Star, *18 Dec 1945*

WHAT'S WRONG WITH THIS ONE?

ALL NATIONS

*Left. When King first raised the question of a distinctive Canadian flag he meant the Red Ensign, the flag under which the Canadian forces had fought. He arranged to have it flown over the Parliament buildings in the hope that Parliament would adopt it. Many Canadians had other ideas. The great Canadian flag debate was on, and would go on for twenty years. The Vancouver Daily Province, 1 Dec 1945 **Right.** Canadians hoped that future conflicts would be settled by peaceful negotiations conducted by the United Nations, and that war, hatred and distrust would no longer rule the world. The Pacific Tribune, Vancouver, 1945*

PRVÉ MIEROVE VIANOCE

FIRST PEACETIME CHRISTMAS. North Americans celebrated their first peacetime Christmas in six years in relative comfort and prosperity. Families in war-ravaged Europe and Asia were not so lucky. L'Udové Zvesti, *Toronto, 22 Dec 1945*

THE DOOR TO THE UNKNOWN

The cartoonist summed up the feelings of many people at the end of 1945. The Second World War was over, but the introduction of atomic weapons meant that the world faced an uncertain future. The Halifax Herald, *31 Dec 1945*

Prime Ministers of Canada 1915 – 1945

Sir Robert Borden	Conservative	1911 - 1920
Arthur Meighen	Conservative	1920 - 1921
William Lyon Mackenzie King	Liberal	1921 - 1926
Arthur Meighen	Conservative	1926
William Lyon Mackenzie King	Liberal	1926 - 1930
Richard Bedford Bennett	Conservative	1930 - 1935
William Lyon Mackenzie King	Liberal	1935 - 1948

Leaders of the Opposition 1915 – 1945

Wilfrid Laurier	Liberal	1911 - 1919
Daniel Duncan McKenzie (Acting)	Liberal	1919 - 1919
William Lyon Mackenzie King	Liberal	1919 - 1921
Arthur Meighen	Conservative	1921 - 1926
William Lyon Mackenzie King	Liberal	1926
Hugh Guthrie	Conservative	1926 - 1927
Richard Bedford Bennett	Conservative	1927 - 1930
William Lyon Mackenzie King	Liberal	1930 - 1935
Richard Bedford Bennett	Conservative	1935 - 1938
Robert James Manion	Conservative	1938 - 1940
Richard Burpee Hanson	Conservative	1940 - 1943
Gordon Graydon (Acting)	Progressive Conservative	1943 - 1945
John Bracken	Progressive Conservative	1945 - 1948

Bibliography

Books and Articles

Boothe, Jack. *Accent on Axis*. The Vancouver Province, n.d

Boothe, Jack. *Heeling Hitler*. The Vancouver Province, n.d..

Boothe, Jack. *Let's All Join the C.C.F.* Leaside, Ontario, n.d.

Boothe, Jack. *Why Work?* Leaside, Ontario, 1945.

Callan, Les. *The Maple Leaf Scrapbook*. Canadian Army newspaper, Belgium, 1944.

Callan, Les. *Normandy and on – From "D" Day to Victory*. Toronto, Longmans, Green and Co., 1945.

Cameron, S. *The Amos and Andy of Social Credit*. Calgary, 1935

Cameron, S. *Basic Training Daze: Candid Cartoons of You and Me in the Army*. Victoria, 1943

Cameron, Stew. *No Matter How Thin You Slice It*. Calgary Herald, 1937.

Canada in Khaki. The Calgary Herald, 1917.

Canadian Cartoon and Caricature, Art Gallery of Toronto, 1969.

Canadian Liberal Party pamphlet, 1915.

Canadian Political Cartoons. The Winnipeg Art Gallery, 1977.

Charlebois, Joseph. *Boches*. Montreal, 1915.

Charlebois, J. *La Conscription: tristes dessins et légendes tristes*. Montreal, Éditions du Devoir, July 1917.

Charlebois, J. *La Prohibition: album de caricatures*. [Montreal, 1919?]

Charlebois, J. *Ouerlot Cousineau alias Philomène, aspirant-chef du government de Québec*. Montreal, 1916.

Conrad, Margarette. "The Art of Regional Protest: the Political Cartoons of Donald McRitchie, 1904–1937." *Acadiensis*, autumn 1991.

Coughlin, Bing. *Herbie!* Thomas Nelson and Sons, Canada, 1946.

Coughlin, Bing. *This Army: Maple Leaf Album no. 1*. Canadian Public Relations Group, Rome, 1944.

Coughlin, Bing. *This Army*. Maple Leaf Album, vol. 2, Rome, 1945.

Coutard, Jérôme. *Des valeurs en guerre: presse, propagande et culture de guerre au Québec 1914–1918*. Doctoral thesis, Université Laval, 1999.

Dale, Arch. *The Left and the Right: With Arch Dale of the Winnipeg Free Press*. Winnipeg Free Press, Apr 1945.

Dale, Arch. *$25 a Month: Adventures in Aberhartia with Arch Dale and the Winnipeg Free Press*. Winnipeg Free Press, May 1938.

Dale, Arch. *Five Years of R. B. Bennett with Arch Dale and the Winnipeg Free Press*. Winnipeg Free Press, 1935.

Dempsey, Hugh. *Western Alienation in Perspective*. Calgary, Glenbow Museum, 1981.

Desbarats, Peter and Terry Mosher. *The Hecklers*. Toronto, McClelland and Stewart, 1979.

Duff, Clayton. *Twenty-Five Cartoons on the War*. 1918.

Hancock, Glen. "Robert Chambers: Dean of Cartoonists." *The Atlantic Advocate*, Nov 1981.

Highe, Edward. *Planning for paupers, with due acknowledgment to the authors of the C.C.F. handbook: "Make this your Canada"* [illustrated by Jack Boothe]. Toronto, Forward, 1945.

Kuch, Peter. "Arch Dale: The Pictorial Spokesman of the West," *Historical and Scientific Society of Manitoba*, series 3, no. 19, 1964.

La Palme, Robert. *La Palme: Les 20 premières années du caricaturiste canadien / The first twenty years of the Canadian caricaturist* [English translation by Irène and Charles Spilka]. Montreal, 1950.

La Palme / Norris. Canadian Museum of Caricature, National Archives of Canada, 1997.

Layng, Craig. "Two Centuries of Satire in Canada," *Caricature* 3:2, Aug1991.

Lemay, J. Arthur. *Que Préfères-Tu? Enrôle-Toi! Cette liberté – la tienne – va la défendre outre-mer*. Service de l'information, Ministère des Services Nationaux de Guerre, Ottawa, 1940s.

Levine, Alan G. "Arch Dale and Prairie Politics in the 1930s." *The History and Social Science Teacher*, 22:4, summer 1997.

McCaffrey, Shawn. "Cartoons in the Classroom: R. B. Bennett and the Depression." *Manitoba Social Studies Teachers' Association*, Dec 1992.

McConnell, Newton. *The Knight of the White Feather*. Toronto, 1917.

Nestor, M. S. *Make This Your Canada – And You'll Regret It: Illustrated by Jack Boothe*. Toronto, 1944.

Nichols, T. E. *These Were The Thirties: With Cartoons by the Late Ivan Glassco*. Hamilton Spectator, 1949.

Osborne, Ken. "Teaching About Labour and Industry with Cartoons." *Manitoba Social Studies Teachers' Association*, Mar 1994.

Political Cartoons Reproduced from The Evening Telegram. Toronto, n.d.

Robidoux, Léon A. *Albéric Bourgeois, Caricaturiste*. Montreal, VLB / Mediabec, 1972.

Sandberg, L. Anders and Bill Parenteau. "From Weapons to Symbols of Privilege: Political Cartoons and the Rise and Fall of the Pulpwood Embargo Debate in Nova Scotia, 1923-1933." *Journal of the History of the Atlantic Region*, spring 1997.

Shields, George. *Telegram Political Cartoons*. Toronto, The Evening Telegram, 1923.

Staley, John Edgecumbe. "The Cartoonmen of Canada." *Maclean's Magazine*, Mar 1914.

Trepanier, Leon. *Images d'autrefois: caricatures du pays*, Montreal, La Patrie, 1950.

Trestrail, B. A. *Stand Up and Be Counted: or Sit Still and be Soaked*. Toronto, McClelland and Stewart, 1944.

Vining, Charles [R. T. L.]. *Bigwigs: Canadians Wise and Otherwise; with 37 illustrations by Ivan Glassco*. Toronto, McMillan, c1935.

War Cartoons and Caricatures of the British Commonwealth. Ottawa,

The National Gallery, 1941.

Werthman, William and W. Stewart MacNutt. *Canada in Cartoon.* Fredericton, Brunswick Press, 1967.

World War One Broadside Collection. Metropolitan Toronto Public Library.

Vokey, Scott. "Inspiration or Insurrection or Harmless Humour? Class Politics in the Editorial Cartoons of Three Toronto Newspapers During the Early 1930s." *Labour / Le Travail,* spring 2000.

Periodicals

More than 430 newspapers, magazines and other sources were examined. The cartoons selected came from the following publications:
L'Action Catholique, Que.; *L'Action Libérale,* Mont.; *The Alberta Non-Partisan,* Calgary; *The Albertan,* Calgary; *L'Almanach de la Langue Française,* Mont.; *La Bataille,* Mont.; *BC Veteran's Weekly,* Vanc; *La Boussole,* Mont.; *The Brantford Expositor; The British Columbia Federationist,* Vanc.; *The British Columbia Monthly,* Vanc.; *The British Columbian,* New Westminster; *Calgary Eye Opener; The Calgary Herald; Le Canada,* Mont.; *Canadian Labour Defender,* Tor.; *Canadian Labor Press,* Ottawa; *The Canadian Liberal Monthly,* Ottawa; *The Canadian Magazine,* Tor.; *The Canadian Unionist,* Tor.; *Le Canard,* Mont.; *The Chatelaine,* Tor.; *Chez Nous,* Terrebonne, Que.; *The Citizen,* Ottawa; *La Conscription,* Mont.; *The Country Guide and Nor'-West Farmer,* Wpg.; *La Crie de Québec; The Daily Colonist,* Victoria; *The Daily Express,* London; *En Avant!,* Saint-Hyacinthe; *The Evening Telegram,* Tor.; *The Farmer's Sun,* Tor.; *Le Fasciste Canadien,* Mont; *The Financial Post,* Tor.; *The Gazette,* Glace Bay; *The Gazette,* Mont.; *The Goblin,* Tor.; *Le Goglu,* Mont.; *The Grain Growers' Guide,* Wpg.; *The Grit,* Tor.; *The Halifax Chronicle; The Hamilton Spectator; The Halifax Herald; L'Idée Ouvrière,* Saint-Hyacinthe; *John Bull,* London; *Le Jour,* Mont.; *The Labour Leader,* Tor.; *The Leader–Post,* Regina; *Maclean's Magazine,* Tor.; *Manitoba Commonwealth,* Wpg.; *Manitoba Free Press,* Wpg.; *The Manitoba Veteran,* Wpg.; *The Monetary Times,* Tor.; *The Montreal Daily Star; Montreal Witness and Canadian Homestead; La Nation,* Mont.; *Le Nationaliste,* Mont.; *The Nutcracker,* Calgary; *One Big Union Bulletin,* Wpg.; *The Pacific Tribune,* Vanc.; *La Patrie,* Mont.; *La Patrie Dimanche,* Mont.; *Pioneer,* Tor.; *La Presse,* Mont.; *La Province,* Mont.; *Reason,* Tor.; *Saskatchewan Commonwealth,* Regina; *Saturday Night,* Tor.; *The Scoop Shovel,* Wpg.; *The Sentinel and Orange and Protestant Advocate,* Tor.; *Le Siffleux,* Mont.; *Le Soleil,* Que.; *The Standard,* Mont.; *La Terre de Chez Nous,* Mont.; *The Toronto Daily News; The Toronto Daily Star; The Toronto Star Weekly; Toronto World; L'Udové Zvesti,* Tor.; *The Unemployed Worker,* Vanc.; *L'Union,* Mont.; *The Vancouver News Herald; The Vancouver Province; The Vancouver Sun; The Vancouver World; The Vernon News; The Veteran,* Tor.; *Victoria Daily Times; La Vie Ouvrière,* Que.; *La Voix du Peuple,* Mont.; *The Weekly News,* Wpg.; *The Western Idea,* Vanc.; *The Western Woman's Weekly,* Vanc.; *The Windsor Daily Star; Winnipeg Free Press; The Winnipeg Tribune; The Worker,* Tor.; *Young Worker,* Tor.

Acknowledgments

Assistance with research was provided by the following institutions: Bibliothèque nationale du Quebec, Montreal (with special thanks to Denise Paquet and Jeannine Rivard); City of Vancouver Archives; Glenbow Archives, Calgary; Legislative Archives of Manitoba, Winnipeg; Legislative Library of Alberta, Edmonton; Metropolitan Toronto Public Library; Ontario Archives, Toronto; Provincial Archives of Alberta, Edmonton; Provincial Archives of British Columbia, Victoria; Provincial Archives of Manitoba, Winnipeg; Public Archives of Canada, Ottawa (with special thanks to Jennifer Devine and Lindsay Stephenson); University of British Columbia, Vancouver; United Church Archives, Toronto; University of Alberta, Edmonton; University of Manitoba, Winnipeg; McGill University, Montreal; Université de Montréal; University of Toronto; University of Victoria; University of Winnipeg; Vancouver Public Library.

Every attempt has been made to trace copyright ownership and credit sources correctly. The authors would be pleased to hear of any errors or omissions. Cartoons by Jack Boothe are reprinted with the permission of Janice Ollson; by Les Callan, Margaret Callan; by Henry Stewart Cameron, Provincial Archives of Alberta; by Robert Chambers, Anita Chambers; by Bruce Hutchison (Pentridge), Robert Hutchison; by Robert La Palme, Jean-Pierre Pilon, Fondation Robert La Palme; by James Reidford, David Reidford; by Hugh Weatherby, *The Daily Colonist,* Victoria. Cartoons by John Collins, Harry Gutkin and E. S. Russenholt are reprinted with the kind permission of the artists.

The authors would like to thank Sigrid Albert, Mildred Fung, Fernand Harvey, Daniel Huzyk, Henry Ivanisko, Andy Jakoy, Yarema Kowalchuk, Adam Kozak, Desmond Morton, Dennis O'Reilly, Gordon Smith and Bill Waiser for their help and advice. The authors would particularly like to acknowledge the invaluable criticism and encouragement of Gordon Smith and Bill Waiser.

Cover

The front cover is based on a cartoon by Les Callan which appeared in *The Vancouver Sun* on December 16, 1929. The cartoon on page vii and on the back cover appeared in *The Canadian Liberal Monthly* on December 14, 1917.

Index